Call the
Final
Witness

Call the Final Witness

The People v. *Darrell R. Mathes*

AS SEEN BY THE ELEVENTH JUROR

Melvyn Bernard Zerman

HARPER & ROW, PUBLISHERS

New York, Hagerstown, San Francisco, London

FIRST EDITION

Designed by Lydia Link

Library of Congress Cataloging in Publication Data

Zerman, Melvyn Bernard.
    Call the final witness.
    1. Mathes, Darrell R. 2. Jury—United States.
I. Title.
KF224.T43Z47   345′.73′02523   76–26259
ISBN 0–06–014791–1

77 78 79 80 10 9 8 7 6 5 4 3 2 1

To Miriam, Andy, Jared, and Lenore

Contents

Acknowledgments

IN WRITING THIS BOOK I required not merely the encouragement that served as periodic blood transfusions to an aging first-time author, but also the guidance and advice that steered me successfully through the thickets of our legal and correctional system. And I needed a great deal of other help as well. To *all* those who provided aid, comfort, and direction I offer here my deepest appreciation; there are, however, some I must single out.

First of all, from home, my wife, Miriam, and my children, especially Lenore, who is so adept at deciphering words mumbled into a tape recorder that, if all else fails, she should have a future with the CIA; from San Francisco, Susan Frankle; from St. Albans, the family of the real Darrell Mathes, particularly his father and his eldest sister; from state and city agencies, Thomas Demacus, Roger Casey, John P. Walsh, and, especially, Captain Brendan Nash; from the media, Ira Silverman, George Dessart, and Marjory Aronson; from various law offices, Carl Rachlin, Sidney and Robert Sparrow, Ken Kirschner, Mary Alice McCrimons, Maureen Crescimano, Edith Rosenthal, and Ethel Grenetz; from Harper & Row, Virginia Mangan, James Fox, Marge Horvitz, and Alice Kenner.

I can never sufficiently thank Leroy B. Kellam and Stephen J. Singer, whose contributions to this book should be dramatically evident to anyone who reads it. I can only say that my debt to them is beyond legal fees.

Finally, to Joan Kahn I offer all the gratitude an insecure

author can bestow upon his editor. Her skill and judgment as well as her friendship and her faith were essential to the creation of this book.

To cite the real Darrell Mathes in the context of acknowledgments seems to me both inadequate and inappropriate. He is, in more than one sense, my collaborator. And so I will state here, as I repeat later, only one indisputable fact: without his deep commitment to this project, and to me, there, quite simply, could be no book.

Author's Note

ALL THE EVENTS of this book actually happened exactly as described. However, because jurors are not permitted to take notes in the courtroom or the jury room, I was forced to trust my memory for the testimony, comments, conversations, and all other verbal statements that I present as direct quotations in the Journal of a Juror. Since the journal was written in the evening of each day of the trial, I consider my memory to be reliable, yielding at best, and in many instances, verbatim accuracy; at worst, and in a few instances, approximate paraphrase that captures the meaning a speaker intended, if not his or her exact words. New York's budgetary restraints have dictated that transcripts of trials be printed only upon the order of the court or at the request of the prosecution or defense. After the trial of *The People* v. *Darrell R. Mathes* no such order or request was made and therefore I was unable to check my reconstruction of the courtroom proceedings against a written transcript.

To protect the privacy of the people concerned, I have changed the names of the defendant, his family, various prosecution witnesses, and certain persons referred to in testimony, and I have scrambled the numbers of all the jurors except myself. I have further disguised the identities of certain jurors by departing from fact in their physical description and in the details of their background. It is my firm belief, and my enduring intention, that no reader of this book should be able to discover or even surmise the real-life identity of any of the jurors, with the exception of Juror 11.

In the non-journal sections of this book the words of Darrell R. Mathes, members of his family, his attorneys, and others are taken directly from tape recordings, my notes, or other documents. While they have been given false names, the defendant, his father, and his brothers and sisters will of course recognize themselves. Perhaps they will be recognized as well by others who are close to them. I hope, however, that this book does not cause serious embarrassment to any member of the family, and I hope, too, that it may in a small way make life better for at least one of them.

Prologue

ON OCTOBER 14, 1974, Edward Fendt, a routeman for the Wise Potato Chip Company, was murdered, probably a few moments before 5 P.M. He had just made delivery to a grocery store in the St. Albans section of Queens, New York City, and he was climbing into his van when someone apparently came up behind him, gun in hand, and attempted a holdup. Fendt was armed and resisted. This was his undoing, for he was then shot at least five times: three bullets lodged in his stomach, one tore through his left arm, and one pierced his skull and brain, killing him instantly.

About a half hour later and no more than six blocks away, Ricky Mathes sat down to dinner in the kitchen of his one-family house. He had turned sixteen just three days before. As his mother served the meal, she told him that she was very sick and probably would not live much longer.

One year later, on October 14, 1975, at 4:45 P.M., within minutes of the anniversary of Edward Fendt's murder, I was selected to be the eleventh juror in the trial of Fendt's accused killer, Ricky Mathes.

This book will cover the police investigation of the crime and what happened to Ricky Mathes during the year between the murder and the opening of the trial. It will also tell of Ricky's life before October 14, 1974. But it will concentrate on the eight days of the trial, the events in the courtroom as seen from the limited perspective of a juror, and the deliberations in the jury room as seen from the full perspective of a participant.

I had been called for jury duty twice before. The first time, in the early 1960s, is now a blurred memory. I served then, as I did later, at the Queens County (New York) Supreme Court, Criminal Division, in Kew Gardens. For four boring days that began at about 9:30 A.M. and ended anywhere between 3 P.M. and 4:30 P.M., I sat on a bench in a large, ugly room, reading, engaging in desultory conversation with other potential jurors, and waiting for my name to be picked out of a drum.

It was Friday, the fifth day, and sometime before noon, when I was finally "paged." I recall few details of the trial or the crime. But I know that the *voir dire* (the questioning of prospective jurors and the elimination of those who appear prejudiced to either judge, defense, or prosecution) was relatively swift and painless, and before 2 P.M. the twelve of us who had been selected for the jury, and two alternates, were escorted to a restaurant across the street from the courthouse for lunch.

We started hearing testimony as soon as we returned to the courtroom. The defendant was accused of forgery—he had allegedly signed his employer's name to a check—but I can remember no more than that, except that the person who should have been the key witness against him was not called to the stand. Testimony lasted less than three hours, and when it was completed, I recall that the judge asked us if we wished to start our deliberations immediately or wait until Monday morning. We chose the former, were in the jury room by 6 P.M., and delivered our verdict, not guilty, before eight. Since it took us the better part of two hours to reach a decision, I suppose at least one of us must have had some doubts, but the absence of that key witness fatally weakened the state's case, and with the same relative ease that we had been chosen for the jury, we came to our unanimous conclusion. I remember that in those halcyon days of municipal affluence, after the verdict was announced the court offered to buy us all dinner as a gesture of appreciation for our services. And I remember, too, that, while I had to get home because we were expecting guests, almost all the other jurors accepted the invitation.

Because I had served on that one-day trial, I was excused from jury duty for the customary second week. And it was then close to ten years before I was called for jury duty again. It was the first week of March, 1972: I remember reading of Senator Edmund Muskie's disappointing showing in the New Hampshire primary as I sat in that same large, ugly room in the Queens County Supreme Court (it must have been painted at least once in the preceding decade, but it didn't show). This was the third day of my second tour of duty, and not only had my name not yet come up; there had been hardly any rolls of the drum.

Perhaps as a small indication of why the days of municipal affluence are no more, there were hundreds of us in that room and very few cases that could conceivably need us. I would not venture a guess as to how much of the taxpayers' money was squandered on us that week in the Queens County Supreme Court, but by Thursday afternoon somebody up there took pity on us and on the public treasury. We were told that anyone who wanted to leave was officially excused from serving the remainder of his jury duty. I was rather surprised to note that much less than half of the newspaper-readers, cardplayers, conversationalists, and window-gazers who populated the room took advantage of the offer. They looked up and listened while the announcement was being made, but then they went back to what they had been doing. The rest of us left the courthouse, looking forward to receiving our modest checks, little enough to compensate us for four days of doing nothing.

It may be that those who chose to finish out their terms knew something I didn't know. For having served my aborted four days, I did not have to wait another ten years for my next notice from the Queens County Supreme Court. It came much sooner than that. If I had dallied through that second week in 1972, I perhaps would not have been called in 1975 and the Potato Chip Murder Case would have remained a crime I had not read about in the local press.

The notice arrived while I was in California on a business trip. I saw it the night I got home, exactly a week before I was due to report. I knew that I would have no trouble getting a postponement of jury duty. All I had to do was ask for it when I arrived at the courthouse on the appointed day. Both times before and now again I considered requesting a postponement. But a postponement is simply that, and a second postponement is much harder to get than a first. So if I put off service now, I might well be called within the next few months and at a time less convenient than the middle of October. Also, I remembered the excessive number of jurors who served with me in March, 1972. Perhaps again there would be too many of us and I would be excused after only a few days. I decided to take my chances.

Because Monday was Columbus Day, my two-week stint began on a Tuesday. That was the only immediate difference between this and my earlier terms of service. Certainly the place was the same, Queens County Supreme Court, Criminal Division, Kew Gardens, the waiting room was the same, and so was the number of prospective jurors—hundreds. So indeed was my mood, of impatient resignation, as the better part of an hour was consumed in simply calling the roll.

But then, just as soon as that was accomplished and all the people whose names had not been called were properly indentured, one of the guards whirled the drum. Never before in my experience had there been such an instant need for a panel. However, given my past success at the waiting game, I felt it was unlikely that my identification slip would roll out of the barrel. It did.

From this point on the Journal of a Juror takes over, but a few words must be offered first to explain how and why the journal came to be, and once it was, how and why it turned into a book.

Almost as soon as I entered the courtroom on October 14, I sensed that this would be a dramatic case. The *voir dire* was already in its fourth day and only six jurors had been selected. I was one of a group of forty prospective jurors and the challenges to us, from both defense and prosecution, seemed arbitrary and relentless. Objections flew, the judge interrupted frequently, speaking harshly to the attorneys and impatiently, on occasion, to some of us. Already in the courtroom there was the kind of tension that I had previously associated only with trial plays and movies. It was occurring now because a seventeen-year-old boy was on trial for murder, a fact that was repeated incessantly, though for different reasons, by the defense counsel, by the district attorney, and by the court as the interrogations rumbled on. All the while the defendant sat stonily at the defense table, searching the faces of jurors and prospective jurors, saying virtually nothing to his attorneys, unsmiling even when the *voir dire* yielded some comic relief.

Everything, then, that first afternoon combined to emphasize how crucial was the role the jurors would play. And so, when I was finally selected for the jury, shortly before court was recessed for the day, I felt a burden and an excitement that I had not at all foreseen when I had reported to the courthouse that morning. And on my way home I decided to keep a journal of the trial, for no one's eyes but my own.

Why? I was sure I would remember the most important details of the testimony even if I put nothing down on paper. I knew also that all the material submitted in evidence in the course of the trial would be made available to the jury during its deliberations. (I did not know that the judge's charge to the jury would include a fairly detailed review of every witness's testimony.) But I wanted the security of knowing that my decision would be based on *everything* that I considered significant at the time I perceived it. And for me this could come only if at the end of each day I wrote down precisely what my mind retained of that day's proceedings. (The attorneys had several times predicted that the trial would last two weeks and I could not trust my memory to hold so much for so long for so serious a purpose.)

But there was another element that figured in my decision to keep the journal: the enjoyment and the challenge of doing so. I had never kept a diary and I was not a professional writer. (Indeed, the court records will show that I answered negatively when, in the *voir dire*, the prosecuting attorney, knowing that

I worked for a publishing house, asked if I was a writer.) But through no choice of my own, I had been thrust into a dynamic, structured situation, where conflict was total, stripped bare, and over the highest possible stakes. Simply for my own satisfaction I wanted to see whether I could capture the quality of the experience, the excitement of the battle, on paper. If I succeeded at all, sometime in the future, rereading the journal, I could relive the trial and also, with the passage of time, enjoy it as a kind of fiction, with the peculiar pleasures that even imperfect art should hold.

This was my sole intent as I faithfully wrote the journal each night of the first week of the trial. I tried hard to recall every piece of testimony that could eventually affect my final verdict. I recorded the attitudes of the participants as I perceived them. And I inserted observations that were essentially irrelevant to the case (for example, items about prospective jurors who were rejected) just to add "color" to the account, to reconstruct, as best I could, my nonfiction melodrama.

And then, at the end of the trial's fifth day, I saw a wholly new purpose for the journal—and with that purpose came the idea for a book. It was on the fifth day that the crux of the trial stood plainly revealed. The jury would have to decide the fate of a seventeen-year-old boy simply on the credibility of three other teen-agers. There probably would be no other evidence to base a judgment on. How could we determine the truth of what these witnesses were saying when all we had were their words? How could we differentiate between deliberate lies and unintentional lapses of memory or perception? How could we be sure that twelve other intelligent people listening to the identical testimony would not reach a verdict that was just the reverse of ours? How good would this jury prove to be when measured against an objective standard, if such a standard even existed? And if this jury was good, or bad, did it suggest any commentary on the jury system itself?

I had, then, moved the Trial of Ricky Mathes to a higher, more theoretical plane, one that demanded more than the journal I was keeping. For to judge this jury (and of course, this juror), I had to review *all* that we had been told, not merely what I mined from memory in my nightly recall. Only then could I offer an opinion on how rational were our deliberations and how valid, indeed how just, was our verdict. I was not sure whether a transcript of the trial would be available to me (as it turned out, none was ever made), but I was sure that, at the very least, I would be able to reexamine all the evidence that had been introduced. It consisted entirely of either written reports or photographs. There was no gun, no piece of clothing left at the scene of the crime, no marked currency—just words and pictures, all those exhibits that, by the end of the fifth day, we the jury had yet to see. By studying this material again, after the trial was over, in a mood of detachment and in an atmosphere free of tension, I could use the same evidence that had helped decide the fate of the defendant for the purpose of assessing the jury.

But to judge the *jury system* by this jury's performance required even more. On the basis of the journal and a reconsideration of the evidence, this jury could prove to have done well indeed and could stand revealed as totally serious, totally reasonable, totally responsible. On the basis of the truth of the crime, however, it could perhaps prove to have been totally wrong—and there would be the ultimate comment on the jury system.

To search for the truth of the crime I would have to venture into areas from which I as a juror had been barred. I would have to gain access to the files of the defense and prosecuting attorneys in order to determine whether all the facts relevant to the Trial of Ricky Mathes had been presented in court, to learn how each side had shaped and structured its case, to understand the extent, if any, to which the strategies used in pursuit of a guilty or not guilty verdict obfuscated the truth that I now sought.

And in my search I would have to go further than the law. There seemed to me then—and there seems to me today—only one person who knew for certain whether Ricky Mathes was innocent or guilty: the defendant himself. So, if the journal was to become a book and the book was to accomplish all that I now intended, Ricky Mathes's full story would have to be an essential part of it.

Obviously, at that point, the evening of the fifth day of the trial, I did not know whether the idea for this book would ever advance beyond the conceptual stage. I needed the cooperation of the attorneys on both sides and, most important, of the defendant. Would all of them—would any of them—consent to be interviewed? Didn't the answer to this question depend on the outcome of the trial? I put all thought of the book out of my mind until the trial was over.

Eventually, of course, the book was born. To widely varying degrees, I received cooperation from both the district attorney's office and the defense attorneys. And Ricky Mathes agreed to tell me the story of his life. He did so over the course of many hours, his words usually but not always recorded on tape.

A fundamental question: Did Ricky Mathes tell me the truth? In Part Five of this book, along with other observations, opinions, and conclusions, you will find some speculations and a final judgment on this question. They are *my* speculations only, and my final judgment. As you read to the end of the book, you will, I hope, be moved to speculate yourself—and to come to your own conclusions. For whatever the questions in this book, in an absolute sense there are no final answers.

Some vital data about myself are necessary to explain a few personal references in the journal. My wife, Miriam, and I have been married for twenty-three years and have three children: Andy, twenty, now a senior at the University of Michigan; Jared, seventeen, a freshman at the same university; Lenore, fourteen, a sophomore at Forest Hills High School in Queens. They are all mentioned in passing in the book and they are the only ones whose real names I felt free to use without a moment's legal hesitation.

I have been employed for more than sixteen years at a major New York publishing house in a non-editorial capacity.

Although I attended college and graduate school, I offer no intellectual credentials here, for I do not regard myself as an expert in any area related to crime or the law. For the purpose of this book I am just a juror, as any of you may become, or have become, on occasion.

PART ONE

Ricky

RICKY MATHES was born in New York City and has lived there all his life, but by the age of seventeen he had rarely been to Manhattan and had never been to those places that the tourists visit. His New York is primarily a section of eastern Queens called St. Albans. Almost entirely black, it is far from homogeneous in the economic levels it embraces. There are streets in St. Albans of wide, tree-dotted lawns and large, imposing turreted and Tudor houses. There are other streets where the homes, standing on narrow plots, are smaller and plainer, but well kept and securely middle class nonetheless. St. Albans' main thoroughfare, Linden Boulevard, lined with one- and two-story office buildings, churches, schools, and stores, some with apartments above them, seems to be both dying and coming to life. Much of it is shabby and drab—shops boarded up, windows painted over, concrete walls smeared with graffiti, vacant lots choked with weeds and debris. But along Linden Boulevard, too, are bright new storefronts and modern buildings (churches, banks, a center for the NAACP) that bespeak revitalization and recovery. And it is these qualities that are emblazoned in a recent Linden Boulevard landmark: two handsome, vibrantly colorful, joyous murals that decorate the walls of a Long Island Rail Road trestle, over which roar the commuter trains that never stop at St. Albans.

Just off Linden Boulevard, there are some streets of modest one- and two-family dwellings, as close as fingers, and it is on one of these streets that the family of Robert Mathes lives. Their three-story yellow clapboard house is not large (the lot is forty by one hundred feet), but it includes six bedrooms (two in the basement), a living room, dining room, kitchen, enclosed porch, and attic, and has a separate garage. Built about forty years ago, it is a comfortable house, decently furnished, but it betrays a subsistence-level income, or indifference and neglect, in its cracked front steps, its peeling paint both inside and out, its front yard composed of dirt and weeds, its doorbell that no longer works.

Here until the fall of 1974 Ricky Mathes lived with his parents, Robert and Livvie Mathes, his four brothers and three sisters, and his nephew, his eldest sister's year-old son. Ricky is the third youngest in the family. His brothers include Dwayne, then twenty-three; Warren, twenty-one; Joseph, eighteen; and Lewis, eight; his sisters, Penny, twenty; Joanne, seventeen; and Sheila, thirteen. Mrs. Mathes had worked for many years, but in October of 1974 Robert Mathes was the only income-producing member of this unfragmented family, and so he is today. He is proud to say that he owns the house they all live in and that he meets his mortgage payments regularly.

Robert and Livvie Mathes were both born in Buena Vista, Georgia, but they did not meet until they had come north and settled in Brooklyn. Robert arrived in New York in 1943, at the age of seventeen, Livvie sometime later. She was just seventeen when they were married, in 1949; he was twenty-three. Their first son, Dwayne, was born within two years and thereafter the births followed in an almost uniform rhythm of one- or two-year intervals: Warren, Penny, Joseph, Joanne, and then, on October 11, 1958, Darrell Ricky, who has been called Ricky for as long as he can remember.

The family was living at that time in the East New York section of Brooklyn, the scene of Ricky's earliest memories. Surprisingly fond memories they are. Home was an apartment in a tenement in an area that today is a desolate slum and in the early sixties was rapidly degenerating into its present hopelessness. But Ricky speaks of it almost longingly—mainly, it seems, because there were friends no farther away than the other apartments a few steps down the hall. "You didn't have to go *out* to be with other kids. They was there," he recalls.

And in Brooklyn there was action too. Unlike the quiet, almost rural streets of St. Albans, where no high-rise buildings are in sight, East New York qualified then, as now, as an urban jungle. Crowded streets, plenty of kids of all ages, gangs, drugs, crime, traffic, noise. Ricky remembers stealing rides on the back of buses, this before he was six, and today he talks of such incidents in a great burst of enthusiasm and laughter, a rush of words that contrasts sharply with the spare and halting quality of most of his speech.

He remembers that when he was four his best friend—"the best friend I *ever* had"—was a boy of the same age who lived in the apartment directly below the Matheses'. He was called Laddie Boy, a nickname given to him after he was tricked into eating a well-fried hamburger made of the dog food. This is just one of the incidents of a carefree and mischievous early childhood that Ricky recalls gleefully. Of the Brooklyn period of his life he goes on to say:

> We used to have block fights and lot fights against the fellers around the block—not to hurt anyone, just to be throwin'. . . . [My] brothers used to take me to the boulevard and we used to jump on the back of the buses and ride all the way down there and couldn't find our way back. . . . We used to climb up on the fire escape and go through the neighbors' window and [they would] walk in the door from work, we'd say "Boo" and we'd run and hide and run out.
>
> And Laddie Boy's brother—he was about eight at the time—he was a firebug and he used to see these mattresses in old dump yards and he used to set 'em on fire and let 'em burn up and stand there and watch 'em. . . . Laddie Boy's little sister was my girlfriend. My little sister was his girlfriend and his oldest sister was Joe's girlfriend. His brother [the firebug] was Joanne's boyfriend. His other brother was Penny's boyfriend. And

his *other* sister was my oldest brother's girlfriend. So altogether the family was like this [he interlocks his fingers]. Everybody was with somebody for each family. It was a very happy childhood.

But it was not to last. A year before Ricky was born, his father had started working for the New York City Board of Education as an assistant custodian, a job he has had ever since. Coincidentally, the first school he was assigned to, in the Bronx, was the elementary school I attended, though I had graduated long before 1957, when Robert Mathes started working there. At P.S. 80 for only one year, he was then transferred to P.S. 8, less than a mile away, in the Bedford Park section of the Bronx, and there he works today.

By 1964 Robert Mathes, after seven years in a well-paying job, had saved enough money to buy a home of his own, the yellow clapboard house on 201st Place in St. Albans. Ricky was six by then. His father and mother were delighted to leave the tenement in East New York, and today his father speaks proudly of his ability to move his family into a neighborhood of private homes, tall trees, and quiet streets.

But upward mobility did not set so well with his children, at least at first. Most kids resent leaving the friends and neighborhood they have known for a place of strangers, even if those strangers live more comfortably. But for most kids, including most of the Mathes kids, the new place becomes familiar and agreeable just as rapidly as memories of the old neighborhood fade. Not so for Ricky.

He claims now that he has never been as happy in St. Albans as he was in Brooklyn:

Then we moved out to St. Albans and the only reason we liked it—the only reason we really accepted it—was because it [the house] was big and we could run all over the place . . . get lost in the house, get lost runnin' around the corner. . . . [But] it made everybody very sad [to move].

Ricky adds, "I never really took anybody as a real friend" in St. Albans. He has had only "good acquaintances" there, and in recent years, girlfriends, lots of girlfriends.

It was, however, during his early years in St. Albans that Ricky found his one genuine interest. "My life story is basketball," he announces, and while he started "handling and touching a basketball" in Brooklyn, when he was four or five, it was in the backyard of his own home that he actually learned the game. His coach was his mother, who had been the star of her high school basketball team in Buena Vista.

> I started learnin' the game of basketball [from] my mother. . . . I guess I inherited from her. . . . Ever since we moved to St. Albans we put a basket up on the garage. Most likely at the end of the year, every Christmas coming along, we'd get a new basketball. . . . And then we might go down to the park. I learned the whole technique to the game when I was six. . . . [My mother] used to beat me in basketball even when I was thirteen, fourteen, and fifteen. She used to come in the backyard and embarrass me in front of all my friends. . . . That's how it was.

Ricky started school in September, 1965, at P.S. 136. It was his neighborhood school, within easy walking distance from home and almost entirely black. When he reached the third grade, however, he was scooped up into the Board of Education's integration program and transferred to P.S. 29 in College Point, a mostly white school an hour and a half's bus ride away.

Those who decry long-distance busing for integration get no support from Ricky. For him the three hours a day of school-bus travel was fun and the elementary school at the end of the line gave him, he says without qualification, a far better education than the increasingly segregated schools he was to attend later.

While he claims to have done well at P.S. 29, the memories of school days that he speaks of are lean on reading and writing and arithmetic and, perhaps inevitably, rich with fights in the schoolyard, singing in the lunchroom, and playing basketball during recess. The fights, he says, were not racial ones and they did not often involve him. When he did get into an argument that escalated into blows, his opponent was as likely to be black as white and the reasons for the fights were strictly schoolboy traditional: unjust charges that he had fouled the other kid in a basketball maneuver or that he intended to keep the other kid's racing car when "I just wanted to race it against *my* car." One of the children he was most friendly with was a white boy named Matthew, who lived two or three blocks from the school. "I used to go over to his house for lunch all the time."

Ricky's tendency to react with his fists when unfairly accused was not wholly confined to the schoolyard. It exploded in the classroom on an occasion that he recalls to me with a mixture of relish and chagrin. He must have been eleven years old then and his fifth-grade teacher

> had a habit of pickin' the eraser up and throwin' it at people. So she picked the eraser up and she hit me in the head with it. If you wasn't, y'know, payin' attention the way she wanted you to, y'know, she hit you in the head with the eraser. So I wasn't payin' attention the first time—I was talkin'—an' she hit me in the head with the eraser. [The next time] I *was* payin' attention. So I was writin' somethin' in my book and she threw the eraser and hit me around right here somewhere [he points to his right temple]. I got up and I went over and punched her in the stomach. Then she started cryin' and she called on the dean.

The "dean" then called on Ricky's mother, who had to come to school. But, says Ricky, nothing happened, and the teacher "was scared of me after that." He was not to be so fortunate when he erupted the next time, in junior high school.

If there is just a touch of pride in the way Ricky recounts the stomach-punching incident, there is much more pride, and more than just a touch of shyness, in his description of some elementary school musical triumphs. He used to sing in the school bus and in the lunchroom with his sister Joanne and some other kids. They were eventually asked to sing on the stage in the school auditorium. But his achievement with the bongos and the congos was even more impressive.

> I played the bongos for my elementary school graduation. I was playin'—I don't know the name of the song, but it goes "Down in the market . . ."—somethin' like that—and I was playin' the bongos for that. I got a standin' ovation for that. Everybody's parents was there. . . . This was the sixth grade. I got a standin' ovation.

This was the beginning of a varied if brief musical career. By the time Ricky was in his second year of junior high school he was singing in an eight-man combo.

> There was an organ player, a lead guitar player, a bass player, a sax player, a drummer, a tambourine player, a trumpet player, and I, the singer. And we played in Creedmore, we played in Creedmore for charity. . . . We was playin', y'know, the sides that was out. We had really been practicin' for this for a long time. This new side had just came out and we was practicin' to get this one. We had never gotten it really together. And they kept on sayin', "Play 'Get on the good foot, the good foot, the good foot, the good foot, Ma.'" So I gave the signal to Kenneth—that was our bass player—and he gave the thing to the lead player and then we just played "Get on the Good Foot." And we played it and they liked it. And they asked us to come back to Creedmore. But we never came back and I never sung for 'em no more.

While the combo has remained in existence until today, Ricky stayed with it for only five months, leaving not long after the

Creedmore engagement. He cannot really explain why. After playing the guitar, singing, and even writing some songs for the group, he seems simply to have lost interest. "I was shy," he says. "But I *had* a nice voice." Now he sings only for himself, and when he occasionally picks up the guitar, it is just "to fool around with it."

The Edward Bleeker Junior High School (J.H.S. 185) in Flushing, which Ricky entered in the fall of 1971, was also quite a distance from home. But again he did not mind the long bus ride and he knows the school was superior to his neighborhood junior high. At that time, according to Ricky, 185 had just about an equal enrollment of black and white students although, as in elementary school, almost all the teachers were white.

For a boy as interested in sports as Ricky says he is ("I play all sports. . . . I could play everything. The only thing, I might have played soccer a little bit, but I don't like playing soccer. . . . I don't like being kicked . . ."), junior high provided his first real opportunity to participate in organized athletics. He did make the 185 handball team, but the surprising fact is that Ricky did not even try out for the school basketball team. Today he tries to sidestep the question of why: "I don't think I had a reason why." Then, at my insistence, he speculates, "Maybe I was too short." In any case, outside of school, he assures me, he was on a neighborhood basketball team and he played catcher in sandlot baseball on a church team. And of course, all the while he was playing basketball in the backyard, frequently with his mother, and in local parks with his father and whatever kids were around.

As his first year in junior high was coming to an end, his brother Joseph, then sixteen, was picked up by the police in a strange episode that, for Ricky, was to have repercussions more than two years later. On May 15, 1972, Mrs. Bessie Green, proprietor of a laundromat on Linden Boulevard, swore out a warrant for Joseph's arrest on charges of "reckless endangerment and harassment." She accused him, in the language of the complaint, of pointing "a gun at [her] and her family at her residence"—an apartment above the laundromat—"thereby creating a substantial risk of serious injury to [her] and other members of her family. The defendant, when told to desist, refused and did shout loud and abusive language at the Deponent [Mrs. Green]."

Both charges were later dropped. Ricky says he has no knowledge of the circumstances leading to the complaint or the reasons it was eventually withdrawn. Indeed, the incident itself is hazy in his memory and when, in the fall of 1974, it became important to him, he had to be reminded of it by others.

Less than a year after Joseph's arrest it was Ricky himself who was in trouble with authority, and as a result, his integrated education came to an end abruptly. In the eighth grade he got into another fight with a teacher and this time, rather than nothing happening, he was expelled from the Flushing junior high school. His memory of the incident is vivid and detailed and, ultimately, sad. But his account of it, like his story of the outburst in fifth grade, is laced with irrepressible laughter. It begins with a related incident involving another student.

In junior high school, the science class—I forgot the teacher's name, but he was old. And somebody said, "Pass me my book. Pass me my book." I wouldn't pass it to him . . . 'cause I was readin' it. And he reached for it and I closed it and I threw it at him and hit him in the face. He got up and we started fightin'. So the teacher sent us down to the dean's office. I didn't get suspended. I think we had to apologize. . . . He [the other student] was black. Then I got suspended. I came to class late 'cause the bell had rung and when the bell rings if you ain't in the classroom you have to stay after school for a certain amount of time. So the bell rung and I was right next door to the class. . . . I was *comin'* in to the classroom, but the bell rung. I had to stay after school. So after school was out he [an English teacher] took me down to the detention room. . . . I can't think of his name, but I can't forget about detention. Anyway, he took me down to the detention room and he told me to

stay in there until four o'clock. So . . . I told him I
wasn't stayin'. I says, "I'm not stayin' here." So he took
me to the dean and he said to me, "Don't leave the
room. I don't want to get you in any trouble. Don't
leave the room." But he left, and I left. The next
morning I came back and I got suspended . . . for four
or five days. My mother came to school. . . . I punched
that teacher in the face and I got kicked out of that
school.

   After I came back to school . . . he was givin' a
grammar test and I was always good in grammar. . . . I
had this teacher in seventh grade and I used to pass all
his grammar tests. So he gave a grammar test and I
passed—I know I passed the test. And he put me down
for a 57, so I asked him to check me. Y'know, I'm
looking at it [the test paper], seein' this is right and this
is right. I take it up with him: "You marked these wrong
and they're right, right?" He says, "Oh, sit down.
They're wrong." And I punched him in the face. I got
kicked out of the school. Then I went to 59. And that's
where I learned that the school with more white
children is better treatment than the school with black.
It was better teachin' in there 'cause when I got to the
more black school they was teachin' in the eighth grade
what I had learned in this [the white] school in the
seventh grade.

Ricky finished junior high at I.S. 59, an intermediate school
in Springfield Gardens, just south of St. Albans. He was there for
only a few months before graduating and going on to Andrew
Jackson High School, which, like his first elementary school, is
near his home and has a white enrollment that approaches zero.

   Even today, Ricky expresses no regrets over the two teach-
er-punching incidents. Nor does he grant that there may have
been alternative ways of handling these cases of, to him, blatant
injustice. He views the actions of both teachers as indefensible
and he allows of no mitigating circumstances, such as their
misinterpretation of his conduct. All he knows is that he was

treated unfairly, and this was not to be tolerated. He had to fight back and his fist was the only weapon he had.

The personal honesty that will not permit Ricky to pretend to a remorse he does not feel is also reflected on occasion in disarming self-criticism. Speaking of himself as he was at the time of his expulsion and immediately afterward—as, approaching the age of fifteen, he was about to enter high school—he says, "I was spoiled . . . I know I was spoiled. I was a brat."

Elaborating on the statement, he explains that his mother favored him over his older brothers and sisters, if not his younger. Time, and love, may have enhanced Ricky's memories of his mother's generosity, but there is truth in his smile as he says:

> Most of the time I'd get two dollars at eleven o'clock on a Saturday morning and come back at one o'clock and ask her for five more and she'd give it to me and at night I'd come back and ask her for ten more. And I'd most of the time get it. I was spoiled. . . . Anytime I wanted something I most likely got it and anytime she wanted me to do something . . . I'd do it for her anyway, but she'd say, "Here, take this. . . ."

(One of the things his mother could not get him to do, however, was to go to church. A member of Jehovah's Witnesses, she would have liked Ricky to accompany her to the weekly service and she usually did manage to take along his younger sister and brother. But Ricky "could never get up on time." He did go to church occasionally, particularly when he was staying with relatives in the Bronx, but he favored services that started later in the day.)

Thus, at the age of fourteen, Ricky says now, he had "everything he wanted" except for a motorbike, although he did have to wait a long time for a trumpet, and the clothes his mother insisted on buying for him were far too conservative for his taste. He always had a regular bike—indeed, he claims he was given a new bike almost every year.

> And when I was fourteen I had a bike so pretty
> everybody in the neighborhood wanted to steal it. . . .
> They finally got it. This girl came and asked me for a
> ride and I let her ride it. She came back later on and
> said some dudes took it while she was ridin' it. . . . I
> finally got it back. It was all ripped apart . . . so I put it
> in the garbage can.

Ricky relates this incident with the same extraordinary absence of bitterness—the same bemused acceptance—that stamps his accounts of almost all the other misfortunes, disappointments, and losses of his adolescence. Including, quite definitely, his description of the events leading to his first arrest.

It happened in Brooklyn. Perhaps because he does not like St. Albans "all that much," perhaps because of the mobility—limited in distance but frequent in occurrence—that characterizes life in black communities, Ricky was always spending a few days in South Jamaica (a section of Queens adjacent to St. Albans) or in Brooklyn or in the Bronx, at the homes of various aunts and uncles. Like almost all kids, white and black, he enjoyed "sleeping over" at his cousins', and it was on one such occasion, when he was thirteen, that he had his first confrontation with the law.

He had been staying with an aunt and uncle in East New York and one morning he and his cousin, who was two years older, were riding bikes past a toy factory in the neighborhood.

> We seen some Puerto Rican kids and some other kids
> reachin' through a hole in the window and pullin' out all
> kinds of games and things. . . . My cousin had hopped
> off the bike to see what they was doing. He was lookin'
> and a man drove up to us, and I was circlin' around and
> he stopped me. He said, "All right, child, c'm here." So I
> cut out with the bike. . . . He caught me. When I rode
> off he grabbed the back of the bike. I jumped off the
> bike and he had the bike. Me and my cousin was goin'
> to leave the bikes but we said no 'cause he had just got

a bike stolen over there. We couldn't get two bikes
stolen in the same week. So we came back. . . . No, we
didn't come back. We was goin'. It was funny. They had
called the police and the police was chasin' us. We
hopped in one of the bins, one of the garbage cans, and
the police—they couldn't find us for nothin'. So we was
thinkin' about the bikes . . . and said . . . we had to go
get the bikes. I was gonna come around the corner and
snatch the bikes and go. But they seen me and they
took us down to the station and they told us to come to
court next week.

It turned out, however, that not only were Ricky and his
cousin innocent of the charge of window-breaking; that particular crime had not even been committed. Upon investigation,
the police found that the factory window had already been
broken, and not by any of the kids. While Ricky and his cousin,
who took nothing from the toy factory, were never accused of
theft, the incident was sufficient to get Ricky's name into Family Court records and, of course, to upset the aunt with whom
he was staying. "She was yellin' and screamin' but she didn't do
anythin'. . . . And when I came home, my mother—she was just
yellin' and screamin' too."

To balance such misadventures, Ricky will recall happy
times in his early teens. They were, by and large, the forever
hallowed happy times of boys that age. He spent most of his
summers in Buena Vista, Georgia, his parents' home town. He
would drive down with his parents and brothers and sisters and
there he would visit his paternal grandparents and his maternal
grandmother. Although he says he would not want to live in
Buena Vista, he speaks of his vacations in this small agricultural
town—one hundred miles due south of Atlanta, and about
fifteen miles north of Plains—with an uncommon note of
relaxed affection.

Because of his large family—many uncles, aunts, and cousins as well as his seven brothers and sisters—the major holidays
were occasions of enormous celebration. "Thanksgiving din-

ner," he remarks, with a brand of natural humor all too rarely expressed, "was usually at *everybody's* house." By which he means that on any one Thanksgiving there was some house-hopping among the different branches of the family and also that his mother and certain aunts would alternate in preparing the dinner in different years. And Christmas was "the works" —presents for everybody, the traditional feast, and a tree that his sisters insisted on decorating by themselves. But, he adds proudly, when they bought an artificial tree only he could figure out how to put it together.

Of birthdays, Ricky says, "I like other kids' birthday parties. I don't like my own. They don't turn out right." He had his last party when he was nine, but in later years he "always got a nice big cake" just for the family.

Ricky's fifteenth birthday was approaching when, in September of 1973, he entered Andrew Jackson High School. It's a bad school, as Ricky would be among the first to admit. I asked him once what he would do to change Jackson if he were head of the Board of Education and had at his disposal all the money he could possibly want. His answer was as brief as his solution is unrealizable: "I'd change the kids."

Certainly it is the kids rather than the teachers (of whom only his gym teacher was black) or the courses that Ricky dwells on when he speaks of his aborted high school career. "In elementary school and junior high school I did very well all the time," he claims. "I got good marks all the time, all the time . . . but then Jackson came and too many people there would say, 'Yo Ricky, yo Ricky, yo Ricky,' and then I started messin' up."

"Messin' up" meant cutting classes and playing hooky, which Ricky was doing constantly at Jackson. When asked if he would have fared better at a school that was half white rather than all black, Ricky does not answer in integration terms:

> I think if I had been goin' to a school *away from home* I could do a whole lot better. Away from St. Albans, where people knew me . . . [I was easily influenced]

towards, y'know, "Let's go see some girls. Yeah." "Let's
go play some basketball." "Let's get out and play some
handball in the back." "Let's go play some cards." "Let's
go to the barbecue place." That's how I am.

So Ricky blames himself for his dismal beginning in high
school. His inability to ignore the obvious lures that were continually thrown at him, his need to "bite," caused him to be
hooked day after empty day. He says that his tempters were not
friends—they were just kids he knew. He insists further that
none of them were on drugs. Nor was he. But they were ad-
dicted to the pleasures of street life, to the exclusion of virtually
all else, and Ricky rushed to follow them.

He believes that Jackson High, with all its disorder and
disciplinary collapse—"a lot of teachers got punched in the
mouth" (but none by Ricky)—could offer a decent education to
a student serious enough to seek it. Such a student, however,
would have to actively resist the pressures exerted on him,
would indeed have to fight back—although not necessarily with
his fists. But Ricky—spoiled by parents, unchallenged by school,
complacent by nature—was ready to fight only when he was
unjustly accused. And he heard no injustice in the call to run.

He was running more and more to girls. He had had girlfriends since he was five, but when he reached fifteen they
seem almost to have become an obsession. Laura, Kathleen,
Zara, Lynn, Nicey—he calls the roll of names commonplace and
exotic. But while he was in the ninth grade he met the one girl,
Lala, who today means the most to him. About a year and a half
younger than Ricky, demure and strikingly pretty, she is the
only daughter of parents with fiercely held middle-class values.
She did not then, and does not now, attend Jackson. Ricky met
her in the park, an encounter that, in retrospect, seems to have
been the only good thing that happened to him during that first
year of high school.

On at least one occasion his socializing got him into trouble:
some of the kids he knew took him along to an impromptu party
at the home of a girl named Jennifer Knox. There was dancing

and horsing around and somehow Ricky managed, with the enthusiastic assistance of another boy, to break the arm of a chair. Neither Jennifer, nor her mother, a Mrs. Custis, nor her half-sister Clarissa seemed to mind, and Ricky thought nothing of it at the time. (Far more exciting was the sudden disruption of the party that occurred when Jennifer had to rush her younger brother to a hospital after he got bitten by a dog.)

In all probability, he was scarcely more concerned when, in June of 1974, his first year of high school completed, he received his final grades. He had failed two courses and had not distinguished himself in any. But, not yet sixteen and no more than five feet seven and a half inches tall, he still had a lot of growing to do. Maybe in the fall there would be another, and a better, beginning.

PART TWO

The Potato Chip Man

Ricky

NEW YORK celebrated Columbus Day on Monday, October 14, 1974, and in Manhattan there was the traditional Italianate parade up Fifth Avenue. At the United Nations that day, the General Assembly voted overwhelmingly to invite the Palestine Liberation Organization to debate the Palestine question. In Washington the federal government opened its case in the main Watergate cover-up trial. In Boston a mob of enraged whites terrorized and, with fists and sticks, battered a Haitian immigrant who, having driven into the "wrong neighborhood," fell victim to the storm of hatred and violence that had erupted when black youngsters were bused to South Boston High School in a court-ordered integration plan. In St. Albans, Ricky Mathes, who had turned sixteen just three days before, was probably interested only in the start of the new basketball season. That was important. His favorite team, of any sport, the New York Knicks, would be playing their opening game against the New Orleans Jazz the following Thursday.

Since schools were closed for the holiday, Ricky, without the slightest qualm, was able to sleep quite late. The new term had not begun any more auspiciously than the last had ended. He already was cutting science and music regularly, because he did not like the teachers, but a legitimate day of no classes was always welcome. He finally got out of bed well past noon. It was a nice day, and after he had dressed and eaten, he went out to play skelly with some kids on the block. (Skelly is a street game too complicated to describe to the uninitiated. Suffice it to say that, with rare exuberance and dynamic skill, Ricky has explained to me exactly how it is played.) Later in the afternoon he decided to stroll over to Cambria Heights Park, about eight blocks from home, to see his girlfriend Lala.

Ricky's recollection of the events of his day is fuzzy and bland but, he feels, with justification, there is no reason why it should be otherwise. For him October 14 was, at least until evening, just an ordinary non-school day and after it had passed, it soon faded in his memory, having dropped into its place in an unending, colorless progression.

So he is not at all sure of the times of his various activities. He thinks it was about two-thirty when he got to the park and there, he says, he divided his time between playing basketball with the kids who were around, none of whose last names he remembers (if he ever knew them), and talking with Lala, her cousin, her brothers, and her friend. They left the park, he believes, shortly after five and he was home by about five-thirty.

His only vivid memory of the day is of having supper that evening. For it was then that his mother told him she was very sick and did not have much longer to live. Ricky continues, "She told me what she wanted me to do. . . . She wanted me to finish school and take care of my little brother and sister."

Her disclosure, to which Ricky reacted without tears, did not come as a wrenching shock to him: "She looked like she was sick enough to be leaving us." And if he did not actually expect it, it was only because "I wasn't thinking no way about something like that."

He wasn't but he easily could have been, for his mother's illness was anything but sudden. Livvie Mathes had been suffering from chronic kidney disease for nine years, since shortly before the birth of her youngest child. During six of those years she had worked in a factory, in Hempstead, Long Island, for the Aurora Company, a manufacturer of toy cars. She brought home plenty of samples and Ricky will offhandedly remark that in those days he had a "closetful" of racing cars, "thousands of 'em."

While she worked, the gradual deterioration of her kidneys continued. In 1972, seven years after her condition first became painfully manifest, she was admitted to Triboro Hospital in Queens. She remained there under treatment for three weeks. Upon her release, she returned to her job at the factory and to keeping a home for her husband and her eight children. She still played basketball in the backyard, she still attended her Jehovah's Witnesses meetings, she still on occasion had to report to school because Ricky and, in all probability, a couple of his brothers had got into trouble.

There is no question that by working and bringing in a regular income, Livvie Mathes made a highly conspicuous contribution to her family's way of living. Because of her, it was possible for them to have a car and a telephone (neither of which they have use of today: the telephone is gone and the car sits in the garage, in need of a motor job), and for Ricky to have a new bike almost every year and the two-, five-, and ten-dollar handouts on Saturdays.

But in the spring of 1974 her sickness at last put an end to all that. She entered Jamaica Hospital in May and when she was released, after five weeks of treatment, she was physically incapable of returning to work. Neither her husband nor her son made their usual trip to Buena Vista that summer, but she went, alone, for fourteen days, and for the last time.

Early in the fall, Robert Mathes recalls, he paid four hundred dollars toward having a specialist in renal diseases fly in from San Francisco "just to tell me she wasn't going to live." In all likelihood, Livvie Mathes did not need a physician's report to enlighten her as to the terminal state of her illness. By the middle of October she was preparing her family for her death and trying to preserve her influence on them in a future she would not know.

On October 16 she entered Queens General Hospital. Her mother and her niece came up from Buena Vista. They and her New York relatives and, of course, her husband and children saw to it that she never lacked for visitors. "Somebody was up there every day, all the time," Ricky remembers. "I was there on the seventeenth, then the twentieth, and then every other day."

October stretched into November, and while there was no

chance that Livvie Mathes would recover, by the early days of that month, after three weeks on the "kidney machine," apparently her condition had stabilized sufficiently for there to be talk of her going home. Perhaps the hospital simply could do nothing more for her. In any case, Ricky says, his mother was due to be released in mid-November.

Sometime earlier, probably at the very beginning of November, Ricky had noticed on the wall of a Linden Boulevard delicatessen a reward poster put up by the Wise Potato Chip Company. A thousand dollars was being offered for information leading to the arrest and conviction of the person who had murdered a Wise truckdriver on October 14. Ricky read the poster and remembered it.

At dinnertime on November 11, Robert Mathes was outside working on his car while Ricky was in the kitchen preparing something to eat. It was the first day since Livvie Mathes had entered Queens General that her husband had not by this hour been over to see her. He and Ricky were planning to drive to the hospital after the afternoon visitors got back. It was shortly after six o'clock when they returned. "I seen them coming up the street—my mother-in-law, my sister-in-law, and my niece. I was jackin' up the car," Robert Mathes recalls. "My mother-in-law came over to me. 'Don't worry, Bob,' she said. 'She's gone. She's gone.' " Then, he remembers, he walked onto the driveway at the side of the house, stood for a moment, and sobbed.

The women went inside. Ricky's cousin found him in the kitchen and told him what had happened. He did not cry then but he did later on that night, when he was alone. His mother had died at the age of forty-one.

Death brings out crowds. For the next two days relatives streamed in from out of town. Robert Mathes's mother flew up from Buena Vista, taking her first trip on a plane, which she had vowed she would never do. (But on the day of the funeral she was too overcome to attend the service.) Other relatives drove in from Detroit. In all they filled the Mathes house with more bodies than it can comfortably hold and far more grief than Ricky wanted to hear.

$1000⁰⁰ REWARD

(ONE THOUSAND DOLLARS)

WILL BE PAID TO THE PERSON WHO SUPPLIES INFORMATION LEADING TO THE ARREST AND CONVICTION OF ANY PERSONS INVOLVED IN THE <u>MURDER</u> OF EDWIN FENDT THE "WISE POTATO CHIP" DRIVER WHO WAS <u>SHOT TO DEATH</u> IN HIS TRUCK ON MURDOCK AVE NEAR 201ST ST., HOLLIS N.Y., MONDAY, OCTOBER 14TH AT ABOUT 5:00 P.M.

IF YOU HAVE INFORMATION PLEASE CALL 212-978-7975

ALL INFORMATION WILL BE KEPT CONFIDENTIAL.

On Thursday night there were so many people in the house, relatives as well as others paying their condolences, that Ricky took no notice of a comparative stranger among them. But Lettie Lou Custis, mother of Clarissa and Jennifer, was there. She took notice of him and before she left she found out the time and place of Livvie Mathes's funeral.

Livvie Mathes had died on a Monday. Her funeral was held on Friday, a sunny, pleasant day that turned cold by the time the service was over. After the burial, at Springfield Cemetery in St. Albans, Ricky returned home, but early the next morning he left the house to spend the day at his father's sister's place in South Jamaica. This is his favorite of his "other homes"—he has a cousin there of about the same age—and he went there more than willingly. But on Saturday evening he was traveling again, this time to his uncle's house in the Bronx, to sleep over and to spend some time with his Detroit relatives, before they started their return trip home on Sunday. It was late when he got to the Bronx, but, he remembers, he had a good night's sleep.

Robert Mathes got up very early on Sunday morning, before 6 A.M. He had to retrace Ricky's movements of the day before, driving first to South Jamaica to pick up one visiting brother and then on to the Bronx, to the home of another brother, where Ricky was staying. Left behind in the St. Albans house that Sunday morning were only four of the Mathes children: Joseph and the three girls, Penny, Joanne, and Sheila. And when, shortly after seven o'clock, there was a pounding on the front door, it was one of them who opened it. Three detectives walked in. They had a warrant for the arrest of Darrell R. Mathes.

Penny, the eldest of the kids at home, explained that Ricky was not there. At first the police would not believe her and she remembers one of the cops saying, "If you don't turn him in, the first sign of him we're gonna shoot him." After an energetic but futile search of the house, the police accepted Penny's word. She then told them where she thought Ricky was. They asked that she and Joseph lead them to him.

Outside four more policemen and detectives were waiting and three unmarked cars were parked at the curb. Penny and Joseph were put in the second car with the detectives who had come into the house. They drove off to South Jamaica.

Ricky's sister and brother were unaware that on Saturday he had moved on to the Bronx. They found out when they arrived at their aunt's house. The police were not pleased when they had to get back into their cars and head for Wickham Avenue.

When he stays in the Bronx, Ricky attends church, and his relatives there go to an early service. So, on that first Sunday morning after his mother's death, he was up and dressed well before eight o'clock. His father had arrived at the Wickham Avenue house even earlier, in plenty of time to go to church with his brother's family, his son, and the six or seven Detroit relatives who had slept there on Saturday night.

It was not yet eight o'clock when the police arrived. Ricky remembers that

> three came in the house. Penny and Joe were with them. They told me I was bein' arrested for the murder of Edward Flynn [the victim's name was Fendt, but "Flynn" was how Ricky heard it], the Wise Potato Chip truckdriver. They gave me my rights. . . . Three cars were parked in front of the house. . . . Two [detectives] were in one car and two were standin' by the cars on the sidewalk. As soon as I come out of the house, the first car drove away. Then they put me in the second car.

Robert Mathes had been upstairs when the police entered and made the arrest. The warrant charged Ricky with three felonies: possession of a weapon, armed robbery, and murder. Signed by Detective William McKinley, who also commanded the arrest party, it went on to state that "on October 14, 1974 at about 5:00 P.M., at 201 Street and Murdock Avenue . . . Darrell Mathes . . . while attempting to forcible [*sic*] take and remove property from a one Edward Fendt . . . did shoot and cause the death of the said Edward Fendt."

But Robert Mathes heard only, "They've come to take Ricky away for killing somebody." His sister-in-law, in tears, had rushed upstairs to tell him what was happening. He was stunned and, literally, speechless. He wanted to say something, but the only words that came to him remained within his head: "It couldn't be. It couldn't be. I buried my wife just two days ago. It couldn't be."

He made his way down the stairs and saw the three detectives standing around his son, surrounded by a houseful of relatives. He still did not speak as one of the detectives, probably McKinley, repeated the charges against Ricky. Then Robert Mathes was asked to come along to the precinct house.

Outside he watched as Ricky and the three detectives got into what was now the lead car. Then he and Penny and Joseph entered the other car with two policemen. Little more than ten minutes were needed to accomplish the arrest, and before eight that Sunday morning, while a good part of New York was still sleeping, the two cars pulled away and drove back to Queens.

In the Sunday-morning stillness, with no sirens blaring, it took less than twenty minutes for the two cars to drive from Wickham Avenue in the north Bronx, near the Westchester County line, to Baisley Boulevard in Jamaica, near the Nassau County line. At the headquarters of the 100th Precinct (today the 113th Precinct), Robert Mathes, Penny, and Joseph followed Ricky into the station house. Once inside, he was soon separated from them and placed in a room by himself, which was then locked from the outside. There he was to remain for the better part of four hours.

At one point not too long after reaching the police station, Robert Mathes was permitted entry into the locked room to have a private conversation with his son. This was his first opportunity to question Ricky about the arrest. He recalls:

> I said to him, "Boy, you tell me what you know about this thing." He answers me, "Daddy, I don't know

nothin' except what I read in the paper." He meant that potato chip sign that they had up in the deli. I know my own boy—and I knew he was tellin' the truth.

From time to time police and detectives would wander into Ricky's room and talk to him. Some of these men he recognized from the neighborhood—detectives who were known on the street as "Jack" and "Jill" and "Hipshot." When asked if, on that Sunday, the police tried to any extent to interrogate him about the crime, Ricky replies, somewhat ambiguously, "Not really." But, he goes on, when his oldest brother, Dwayne, came to the station house sometime during the morning, Ricky asked the police if he could see him and, he claims, they then tried some "bargaining": They would let him visit with Dwayne only if Ricky confessed. "So I said I want to talk to my brother *first* and then I'd decide if I would confess." Ricky is boasting here that he "put one over" on the police, since they did allow him to spend a few minutes with Dwayne and he, of course, never had any intention of confessing. Indeed, he made no statement of any kind.

Once in the precinct house, Detective McKinley's first order of business seems to have been to arrange for a line-up. He informed Ricky and his father that this would soon take place and that they were free to engage legal representation in the meantime. When Robert Mathes answered that he could not afford a lawyer, McKinley ventured that it might be possible to have someone from the Legal Aid Society come down and act as counsel for Ricky, at least during the line-up. Robert Mathes said that would be O.K. Thereupon, two other detectives made calls to the Legal Aid Society, only to be told that since it was a Sunday, no lawyers were available.

Shortly after that, all the Mathes visitors left the police station, with Ricky's father eventually going on to the Queens County Criminal Court Building to arrange for permanent legal counsel. There a judge, promising him "the best lawyer in Queens," assigned the firm of Sparrow, Sparrow, Singer, and Kirschner to the Darrell Mathes case.

Back at the precinct house, about two hours after Ricky

arrived, the line-up was held. The police brought in four supposed eyewitnesses to the crime and five black youths to stand with Ricky under the powerful white lights. Three of the four witnesses—Jennifer Knox, Clarissa Custis, and Jimmy Leland— identified Ricky as the person they had seen leaning into or running from the Wise Potato Chip truck, a gun in his hand, at about five o'clock on the afternoon of October 14.

Of course, the three had already identified Ricky from snapshots, taken of him at his mother's funeral two days before. But just as Ricky had not even been aware that those pictures were being shot, the police photographer having succeeded in concealing himself, so Ricky was not soon to learn that it was this trio of teen-agers, all of whom he knew, who had identified him in the line-up. Nor would he find out until much later that Clare Anderson, the fourth supposed eyewitness, had failed to identify him.

The line-up proceeding completed, Ricky was returned to the locked room. He alleges that at this point the police told him "five or six people" had identified him as the murderer and, therefore, he had "better confess." He refused. He was then asked a series of vital-statistic-type questions and, for the first time that day, put in handcuffs. Thus shackled, he was led out of the precinct house and driven to Queens Central Booking, the 112th Precinct in Forest Hills.

At the station house Ricky was placed in a cell with three other men, and there he waited during the course of being "processed." He was fingerprinted, photographed for "mug shots," and measured; samples of his signature were taken. That same day the police sent his fingerprints on to the Latent Section with a request that they be compared with the prints lifted from the Wise Potato Chip van. The next day it was to be reported that identification could not be made.

Ricky remained at Central Booking until well into the evening, before going on to the next way station on his long Sunday journey, the Queens County Criminal Court Building in Kew Gardens. When he was brought into a courtroom, he immediately saw his father waiting, along with his father's brother and sister and her husband. They had been there for a long time.

Also waiting was Ricky's court-appointed counsel, Stephen J. Singer. Their first meeting was brief and allowed no time for them to be alone. They stood at the bar; Ricky pleaded not guilty and was remanded to the New York City Adolescent Reception Detention Center (ARDC), on Rikers Island. The day was almost over as Robert Mathes, with tears in his eyes, watched his son being led from the courtroom.

The Journal of a Juror

Tuesday, October 14, 1975

THE FIRST DAY

UNBELIEVABLE. I'm on the first jury impaneled.

My name is drawn from the drum at ten forty-five, about fifteen minutes after the roll call is finally completed. In all, forty names are chosen, and mine must be about the twenty-eighth. We are told that we are being assigned to Supreme Court, Part III, the court of Judge Thomas S. Agresta. The trial is for murder.

After being taken to the third floor, we must wait in a corridor outside Agresta's courtroom for close to half an hour. Then we are ushered into a large paneled room and seated in the spectators' section, just behind the jury box. There is something immediately imposing about the high-ceilinged, windowless courtroom, with its concentration of recessed lights above the judge's bench. It has the solemnity of a temple and the focus of a theater. All the people seem dwarfed, except Agresta, who sits on his stage, and above us all. As the day progresses he looks down at times benignly at the jurors, at times irately at the attorneys, but always he appears tough, wise, detached, even-handed, and totally in control.

Six jurors have already been chosen (two women, four men), and they fill the lower row of the jury box. This is the third day of jury selection and Agresta is clearly impatient. More than

44

once he complains that there is no reason in the world why it should take so long to get a jury for this case. But the attorneys, both defense and prosecution, are constantly reminding us of the reason: a seventeen-year-old boy is on trial for two counts of second-degree murder.

The prosecutor is Assistant District Attorney Bernard Mendelow, in his late thirties, chubby, his full face both cold and cherubic, his manner unemotional and assured.

There are two defense attorneys, who alternate in interrogating each batch of three or four prospective jurors. The older of the two, and the one apparently in charge of the defense, is Leroy Kellam, in his late fifties, black, a big, flamboyant man, with a broad, calculated smile. His approach to the prospective jurors is hearty, boomingly friendly (his first question to almost each person he interrogates is "And how are you today?"), but behind his affability and "down home" speech (he drops his final *g*'s), his distrust of all of us seems to me unmistakable.

The younger attorney is Stephen J. Singer, white—indeed, unusually pale—probably in his early thirties. He is both the youngest of the attorneys and the most detached, precise, and organized. With him it is always evident where a line of questions is leading.

The defendant is Darrell R. Mathes, seventeen, black, skinny, dressed in a beige leisure-suit-type jacket, dark-brown pants, and sneakers. He sits almost immobile and expressionless at the defense table, diagonally opposite the jury box. His long, long legs are stretched taut. He stares at the prospective jurors and appears to be fully attentive to the questioning. But only once during the entire day do his attorneys speak to him and only once does he smile, and then almost grudgingly, though many times comments by Agresta, Kellam, and certain prospective jurors provoke laughter in the courtroom.

After Agresta's opening remarks to the prospective jurors and his directive to the attorneys to "get on with it," the *voir dire* resumes. Here, too, names are drawn from a drum, three or four at a time, and those called move into the jury box to the first vacant seats in the upper row. Mendelow always interrogates first, addressing each person by name. He asks almost everyone, "How do you feel about serving on a murder trial jury?" and almost everyone answers, "Nervous." Far more often than either of the defense attorneys, Mendelow in the course of his questioning tells us why we are here: "Did you read any newspaper accounts of what came to be known as the 'Potato Chip Murder Case'? The crime was committed a year ago. Do you remember hearing anything about it on TV? Do you know the defendant, Darrell Mathes, or anyone in his family? Did you know Edward Fendt or anyone who works for the Wise Potato Chip Company? Are you familiar with the neighborhood around Murdock Avenue and 201st Street?" From Mendelow's questions alone the broad outline of the case becomes clear.

With all the prospective jurors Mendelow delves into two essential areas: excessive sympathy for the seventeen-year-old defendant, particularly from jurors who have teen-age children, and excessive hostility to the police. His interrogations are relatively brief, mechanical—as if he has done this too often before—but effective in that he leaves no one in the jury box who, at least on the surface, appears prejudiced in the defendant's favor. By peremptory challenge [challenge without stated cause] , he dismisses every black woman and every black man.

There are about eight blacks in our group of forty and all but one of them are called into the jury box before I am. A few are obvious challenges: two people who live near the scene of the crime and know the area well, a man whose wife was recently arrested for trespassing (but soon released), a woman who admits that the state would have to prove the defendant guilty beyond *any* doubt before she would vote to convict. But others, particularly a very conservatively dressed black businessman, seem the epitome of white-middle-class values. They are the targets of Mendelow's challenges all the same.

One question that Mendelow frequently asks seems to me curious and ill-advised: "Some of the state's witnesses may have, shall we say, unsavory pasts. Would this influence you in accepting their testimony as truth?" Of course everyone answers "No" to this or "Not necessarily," but is it wise for the prosecutor to implant seeds of doubt in the credibility of his own case?

When Mendelow has finished his questioning of each group, but before he has revealed his challenges, Kellam or Singer takes over. The black attorney's style is circuitous, deceptive. All that good humor and the seemingly extraneous questions are obviously designed to expose what the prospective juror is like as a person, not simply what he believes. Literally and figuratively, Kellam circles around, but when he detects a soft spot, his questions are quick and, frequently, unfriendly. He challenges the prospective jurors to spar with him and many do. He gets one woman to admit that she thinks the state must have a pretty strong case merely to put a defendant on trial. Kellam (icily): "You believe that, without having heard one word of the state's case against this boy?" Woman (defiantly): "Yes." Kellam (after a long pause and breaking into that wide smile): "You really want to serve on this jury, don't you?" Woman (softly and smiling too): "Yes." To my surprise, Kellam does not challenge her, and she becomes Juror 10. Evidently he found something in her earlier answers that appealed to him.

To most of the others who appear to have a pro-prosecution bias Kellam is much less kind. And he gives short shrift to those who have been, or been close to, the victims of violent crimes. One prospective juror had a child who was murdered, another a neighbor. Even here in a courtroom such revelations have a shock effect, and after he has heard them, Kellam scarcely bothers to question the people further.

Singer's approach, as compared to Kellam's, is subdued, direct, highly structured. He probes for the self-incriminating statement and when the prospective juror provides it, Singer, turning to the judge and asking that the person be excused for cause, has an air not of triumph, but of resigned satisfaction that the inevitable has come to pass. He continually seeks out, and frequently finds, one damaging preconception: That the defense is obligated to "do something" for the defendant—that simply exposing the state's case as not proved beyond a reasonable doubt is not good enough. There are some prospective jurors who acknowledge that the defendant's failure to testify in his own behalf would act as a suggestion of guilt and, indeed, there are others who confirm Singer's suspicion that, deep down, they believe the defense must *prove* their client innocent. Singer is adept at uncovering all these prejudgments, and all of them are of course fatal to the persons' chances of serving on the jury.

That so many should hold these views—and admit to holding them—is, to me, strange and surprising. For as each group of three or four take their seats in the back row of the jury box, the judge instructs them in some basic concepts of the law: an indictment is not an indication of guilt, the defense attorneys do not have to *prove* anything, the burden of proof rests with the state. Those of us who have to wait until late in the day to be called into the jury box hear Agresta's restatement of these principles eight, nine, ten times. Nevertheless, each time it is followed by at least one answer that shows a person cannot or will not subscribe to our ground rules of justice.

No doubt partly because of this, Agresta grows progressively more displeased as the day wears on. He accuses the attorneys of excessive and unnecessary questioning and is forever admonishing them to "get on with it." More than once his impatience, indeed his anger, is directed toward a prospective juror. One poor man, inarticulate from the first, is tied into knots by Kellam, perhaps inadvertently, more likely deliberately. The lawyer finally asks him a question riddled with negatives: "If the state fails to present proof of guilt beyond a reasonable doubt, would you vote for a 'not guilty' verdict?" Answer: "No." Kellam repeats the question, but prefaces it with "Now listen carefully. I don't think you get my meanin'." The negatives are still there, in the question and in the answer. Again and again Kellam restates the question, but always to the same response. Shrugging his shoulders, he turns resignedly to the judge. Agresta rephrases the question slightly but retains the negatives. Again the "No." Agresta's voice rises: "For the last time, if the district attorney does not prove guilt beyond a reasonable doubt, would you find the defendant not guilty?" "No." There's laughter in the courtroom now. The prospective juror is himself smiling foolishly as Agresta growls, "You're excused. Return to the jury room downstairs."

There are others who are excused by the judge, both before and after the attorneys have questioned them: A man who, when he is called to enter the jury box, announces that he is already biased, just from what he has observed while sitting in the courtroom (presumably he is referring to Kellam's aggressive tactics). A very genial man who is now retired from a job in the New York City Corporation Counsel's office. A spry old man who admits to being over seventy years old. A young woman of no more than twenty-three with her right arm in a cast who, after some hesitation, confesses that, yes, she might get very uncomfortable if she were confined to a jury box for two weeks. Agresta lets them all go and several others as well.

It is four-thirty. The *voir dire* has been going on since eleven-thirty, with an hour off for lunch, and only four jurors have been chosen. Juror 7, a homemaker, around fifty, is much less tense and eager than most of us. She answers questions quickly, coolly, confidently, and she gets a laugh at the end of the following exchange:

Mendelow: "How old is your daughter?"

Juror 7: "Twenty-three."

Mendelow: "Is she now employed?"

Juror 7: "No."

Mendelow: "Did she go to college?"

Juror 7: "Yes."

Mendelow: "What did she study?"

Juror 7: "Everything."

Juror 8, who works at JFK Airport, is about forty, a proper fellow whose replies are clearly meant to suggest that beneath his buttoned-up appearance, complete with collar pin, dwells a knowing if not cynical sophisticate. He and Kellam indulge in much by-play, including:

Kellam: "Could you believe that a witness while under oath might lie?"

Juror 8: "Nobody's perfect."

Juror 8 also expresses the view that a trial is a kind of game in which the opposing sides are battling not for justice, but simply for victory. Because of his smart-ass answers, I am mildly surprised that Kellam allows him to serve. But Juror 8 is quite plainly delighted.

Juror 9 is a pleasant, quick-witted woman, in her late thirties, also a homemaker, who, I thought, answered every question "correctly."

Juror 10 is the slightly rattled woman who believes that the district attorney must have an exceptionally strong case in order to get an indictment. She is probably as astonished as I am that Kellam does not challenge her.

Although it is now four-thirty, not a word has been said about court's recessing for the day. My name is called, one of a group of three. We enter the jury box, leaving behind in the spectator section no more than eight of our original panel of forty. Agresta makes his usual statement, asks us about prior jury service. I am one of very few prospective jurors who have served on a criminal case before.

My group includes the black man whose wife was arrested about a year ago for trespassing. Once he has elicited that fact, Mendelow asks him few further questions. He then turns to me, asks me three or four questions about my work, a few more about my family. After learning that I work for a publishing house, he asks if I am a writer and I answer that the nature of my job does not in any way involve writing. Then he focuses on the ages of Andy and Jared and asks if the fact that my two sons are teenagers would perhaps make me overly sympathetic to the defendant. I reply that it would not. He asks me nothing else.

Kellam comes bounding over to the jury box. The big smile. The jovial "And how are you today?"—though weariness has settled over almost everyone. The pleasantries concluded, he begins.

Kellam: "Mr. Zerman, are you familiar with the phrase—it is used a lot in the *Daily News*—'turnstile justice'?"*

M.Z.: "Yes, I am."

Kellam: "And no doubt you don't approve of turnstile justice."

---

*"Turnstile justice" refers to the brief or suspended sentences and/or the plea bargaining that return convicted criminals to the street shortly after they have been arrested.

M.Z.: "No, I don't."

Kellam: "Would you let your feeling about turnstile justice influence your verdict in this case?"

M.Z.: "No."

Kellam: "You wouldn't let the idea of turnstile justice affect your thinking in the slightest."

M.Z.: "No; if the state couldn't prove its case—"

Kellam (interrupting): "Beyond a reasonable doubt."

M.Z.: "—beyond a reasonable doubt, I'd find the defendant not guilty."

Kellam: "And conversely, if the state did prove its case beyond a reasonable doubt, you'd find him guilty."

M.Z.: "Absolutely."

Kellam: "No further questions."

Again unbelievable. Not one person that day has been asked so few questions by the attorneys. And I am not challenged. I move into the seat just vacated by the man whose wife was arrested for trespassing. I'm the eleventh juror, chosen at four forty-five.

The next prospective juror, at twenty-two probably the youngest in our panel and the only one with a beard, is questioned briefly and excused by Mendelow, no doubt because of his age and facial hair. His job at A&S [Abraham & Straus, a Brooklyn department store] is not sufficient to offset the hint of mod.

It's about five o'clock when Juror 12 is finally selected. Slightly built, quiet, about thirty, he, too, works at JFK. He answers questions laconically, almost tentatively, but with persuasive honesty. He is not asked very many, perhaps because it is so late. When he is not challenged, the relief in the courtroom is almost palpable.

But since Agresta is determined to try to complete jury selection today, the *voir dire* continues: two alternates are still to be chosen. The clerk calls four candidates from the eight remaining in the spectator section. Two are questioned: the last of the blacks in the panel and the young girl with her arm in a cast. Both are soon rejected. Two remain in the jury box, but it is now almost five-fifteen and Agresta, wearily shaking his head, acknowledges that it cannot be done. With an admonition that we will undoubtedly hear many times—not to discuss this case among ourselves or with our families, not to visit the scene of the crime—he dismisses us for the day. We are to return tomorrow at nine-thirty, when, he is sure, two alternate jurors will quickly be chosen and we will begin to hear testimony.

On the way home I decide to keep this journal.

Wednesday, October 15, 1975

THE SECOND DAY

We are led into the courtroom at 10:10 A.M. The prospective alternates left over from yesterday are interrogated and accepted so swiftly that I'm amazed. It takes less than ten minutes for Mendelow and Kellam to pose a few perfunctory questions and to get a few perfunctory replies. What is also surprising, and wryly amusing, is that the alternates are like carbon copies of one another. Both are about fifty, Italian, roly-poly types. Both are blue-collar workers, though the first alternate is at present unemployed.

The trial begins. Mendelow, matter-of-fact, solemn, makes his opening statement. In many ways it is a restatement, for his *voir dire* questions clearly suggested the outline of evidence that he offers us now. He gives us some details of the crime and mentions the witnesses the state will call: police types all, except for three eyewitnesses—Jennifer Knox, Clarissa Custis, and Jimmy Leland. He discloses that it took a month for the eyewitnesses to come forward with information that led to the arrest of Darrell Mathes, but he warns us not to be influenced by this fact. As he did yesterday with his references to witnesses' "unsavory pasts," Mendelow is clearly trying to anticipate factors that could weaken the persuasiveness of the state's case. By so deliberately drawing our attention to them, he hopes to reduce their impact. It seems a rather naïve tactic to me.

He ends his statement with a ringing promise to prove Darrell Mathes guilty beyond a reasonable doubt, to demonstrate this so conclusively that we, with all our sophistication and intelligence, will have no choice but to convict the defendant as charged.

Singer makes the opening statement for the defense. His approach is much less solemn than Mendelow's, but he is no less self-assured. His presentation is brief, well-structured: The defense case will follow two paths to a single destination: the state's total inability to prove the defendant guilty of murder. First, the defense will show that the police work in this case was incredibly sloppy, marked by a desperate need to solve the crime; and second, it will show that the so-called eyewitnesses are far less than trustworthy. Singer, too, concludes with a prediction: We will find Darrell Mathes innocent.

Mendelow calls his first witness, a man named Young. He is the deceased's brother-in-law and he testifies that he identified the body of Edward Fendt at the morgue on October 15, 1974, the day after the murder. There is no cross-examination.

The state's second witness is Farouk Passwalla, medical examiner. He testifies that he examined the corpse on October 15, 1974, and found five bullet wounds, one each in the head and the arm and three in the stomach. There were exit wounds for the first two but the other three bullets were still lodged in the body. Again there is no cross-examination.

Mendelow's next witness is Patrolman Wieda, the first cop to reach the scene of the crime, at about five past five on October 14. He was responding to a police radio call reporting shots fired at the corner of Murdock Avenue and 201st Street. Wieda testifies that he had to break into the Wise Potato Chip van because all doors were locked. In the back of the van he found Fendt's body sprawled on the floor. Fendt was dead; a revolver later identified as his own was on the floor between his legs. A second gun, not recently fired, was concealed in a potato chip carton on a shelf of the truck, near the body.

After Wieda left the van, he questioned people standing around on the street. One man, unidentified, told him that he saw a black youth about five feet nine inches and 175 pounds running from the truck. He thought the kid may have jumped into a black Buick Riviera which had been parked at the corner of the next block (Murdock Avenue and 202nd Street) and was then immediately driven away.

Wieda wrote up an account of the incident in his daily log but, he testifies, obviously embarrassed, all the papers (five or six) were lost when he was later transferred to a different precinct.

Kellam begins his first cross-examination with the same broad smile and short-lived joviality that he showed to prospective jurors during the *voir dire.* Then he quickly pounces on the missing log. Wieda cannot explain its disappearance. Increasingly uncomfortable, he doesn't even try to, and Kellam, in slightly different ways, repeatedly makes his point: here is the first instance of police inefficiency in the handling of this case.

Kellam's manner softens as he questions Wieda about the statement of the unidentified eyewitness. Once again we hear about the black Buick Riviera, the possible getaway car, a detail Kellam clearly wants the jury to remember. He then enters into evidence the first defense exhibits, "A" and "B," police forms 49 and 61, which Wieda had prepared as a matter of routine. These are brief summaries of the event (presumably less detailed than the missing five or six pages of Wieda's log) and Kellam questions the witness closely about them: how Wieda broke into the van (he had to smash the glass of the front right window), where the bullet holes were, what attempt he made (apparently perfunctory at best) to find eyewitnesses. Kellam's approach is sharp if not antagonistic, and before he concludes, with "I have no further questions," he has succeeded in revealing Wieda as an ordinary cop responding to a commonplace event with indifferent skill.

The fourth and last witness of the day is Sergeant Palmaccio, Wieda's companion in the patrol car. In answer to Mendelow's questions, he generally corroborates the previous witness's testimony, but he does add a few facts of his own. He testifies that he found a roll of bills, amounting to about two hundred dollars, on a shelf in the rear of the van, near the carton containing Fendt's second gun. After inspecting the truck, Palmaccio went into the grocery store in front of which the van was parked. There he telephoned the forensic squad and homicide detectives. From the owner of the store he learned that Fendt had just made a delivery of potato chips. But the grocer did not offer him any information about the perpetrator.

In his cross-examination Kellam dwells on the number of people who were at the scene of the crime when Palmaccio and Wieda arrived. Palmaccio seems vague on this point, finally says, "About three." He testifies that he did question them, but they revealed nothing of importance. He admits that he didn't ask any of them their names. If Kellam was hoping for testimony reaffirming the report of the Buick Riviera, he is disappointed. Palmaccio says nothing about it. Indeed, he says nothing much about anything. In all, his testimony seems to me rather arid. Who can blame one of the alternates for dozing a bit while Palmaccio is on the stand?

Presumably the police who respond to a radio call are not expected even to attempt a thorough investigation of the crime scene. Certainly Wieda and Palmaccio did not. That is the major conclusion I draw from Kellam's cross-examination of these witnesses.

Palmaccio leaves the stand at four-forty, whereupon court is recessed for the day. As Agresta repeats his admonition, I recall that at lunch today, with Juror 6, we said not a word about the case. Nor was there any mention of it in the jury room. Our respect for Agresta and the ways of justice appears to be complete. But I'm disgruntled by one of the judge's pronouncements: while hearing testimony, the jury is not to be shown any of the evidence introduced by either side. Only after we begin our deliberations will we be permitted to examine exhibits "A" and "B" and "1" and "2" and all the rest. Of course, it is when this evidence relates to the testimony of the witness on the stand that I'm most eager to see it. But I suppose I'll be fortunate if this proves to be the most serious of my frustrations during the Darrell Mathes trial.

Thursday, October 16, 1975

THE THIRD DAY

We the jury have created our own moment of drama. Juror 8, he of the collar pin and the cool (remember "Nobody's perfect"?), did not show up today.

By ten o'clock the judge is ready for us, but Juror 8 has not appeared. The clerk of the court tries repeatedly and futilely to reach him at home. At eleven we are brought into court, only to be told by Agresta that he prefers not to have to use an alternate juror so early in the trial. Therefore, we are dismissed until two-fifteen, in hopes that Juror 8 will show up.

But by two forty-five, when we finally re-enter the courtroom, there is still no sign of him. After we are seated in the jury box, Agresta angrily announces that he has issued a warrant for the man's arrest. He then asks the first alternate to move into the eighth juror's seat and the second alternate to take the seat vacated by the first. This variation of musical chairs accomplished, the trial resumes.

The first witness of the day—and it's now about 3 P.M.—is Detective Robert Willis of the forensic squad. He testifies that in October of 1974 he had had about five years of experience in his current job. He arrived at the murder site at seven forty-five (that was close to three hours after the crime was committed) and proceeded to photograph and "process" the van. When asked to by Mendelow, he defines "process" as a search for physical evidence, including an attempt to "lift" fingerprints. (Fingerprints—perhaps some meaningful evidence at last.) But, he goes on, he found only two usable ones, both on the exterior of the van, on the right door handle and on the right fender. He also found five "deformed" bullets—in his opinion, two from the perpetrator's gun (both on the floor of the van near the rear doors) and three from the deceased's (at left and right front doors and embedded in the partition separating the cab from the rear of the van).

In cross-examination, Kellam moves into the attack immediately. If yesterday he was patronizing to the witnesses, today he is harsh and almost contemptuous. His purpose on both days is the same, however: to demonstrate that the police's search for evidence was halting, superficial, and shockingly inadequate. Again and again he registers astonishment that so few fingerprints were found. With all those potato chip cartons in the back of the truck, how could there be no usable prints on any of them? Did Willis process the cartons? The detective replies that he did, but he adds that cardboard absorbs prints.

Kellam: "How about the steering wheel, then? That doesn't absorb prints. Any fingerprints on the steering wheel?"

Willis: "No."

Kellam: "No fingerprints on the steering wheel. Was the deceased wearing gloves?"

Willis: "I don't recall." (Kellam hands him a photograph of Fendt.) "No."

Kellam: "But you didn't find any fingerprints on the steering wheel."

Willis also admits that he did not notice the deceased's second gun in the potato chip box or the box of ammunition that was nearby. These were found by someone else after the van was taken to the police precinct house. Willis, who seemed uncomfortable throughout much of Kellam's questioning, is visibly relieved when he is allowed to step down.

Mendelow's second witness of the day is Detective William Plifka, who, in response to the assistant district attorney's first question, informs us that he has previously testified in about two hundred trials. Experience tells and he is surely the state's most confident witness thus far.

But his testimony is brief. It is he who analyzed the prints taken by Detective Willis and he found only *one* of them usable. He was then asked to compare that one with the prints of a total of ten individuals. First, in mid-October, he compared the print with those of Edward Fendt and eight early suspects (all named). Then, on November 18, 1974, he compared the print with that of Darrell Mathes (the first time a witness spoke the name of the defendant). All results negative.

Kellam, no doubt pleased that Mendelow ended his direct examination on a note that was emphatically in the defendant's favor, asks Plifka only one question: Had he ever been asked to analyze prints taken from a Buick Riviera? Answer: No.

Thus, if Mendelow's purpose was to show how thorough the police had been in trying to identify their one usable fingerprint, Kellam had undermined him with a single question. Plifka's answer is the last of the day as court recesses early, at four-twenty.

It seems that our new Juror 8 was dozing again, and this time he was apparently caught. As we leave the courthouse, two of the other jurors claim they are certain that Singer brought this catnapping to the attention of the judge, but before Agresta could say anything, Juror 8 awoke. Earlier in the day we had asked Jack, our guard, if we could bring a plug-in coffeepot into the jury room. He denied our request, but certainly it's beyond a reasonable doubt that at least one of us could use a stimulant.

Friday, October 17, 1975

THE FOURTH DAY

As soon as we're all settled in the jury room, Jack, the guard, announces that our former Juror 8 has been found. He didn't show up yesterday because he was sick.

But there is apparently more to the tale than that. Once we are seated in the jury box, just before 10 A.M., Agresta promises to explain to us after the trial is over exactly what happened to the first Juror 8. He makes it sound like a bedtime story to be told by grandpa if we kids are good. I can't believe that an explanation of Juror 8's disappearance would influence our decision.

The first and only witness of the day: Detective William McKinley, built like a halfback gone to fat. Seventeen years in the police department, fourteen as detective, he exudes grit, confidence, and pugnacity. Indeed, in his appearance and demeanor, McKinley could have come straight from Central Casting to take charge of the investigation into the Potato Chip Murder Case. Of the principals, only Kellam is McKinley's equal in looking the part he plays. Agresta is too small in stature, Mendelow too soft in his features, Singer too young and pallid. And Darrell Mathes looks too innocent or not innocent enough, depending on how the director would want the part of the defendant to be played.

Mendelow's direct examination of McKinley is relatively brief. In addition to points already made by previous witnesses, the detective testifies that the police, including McKinley himself, posted reward notices all over the neighborhood of the crime: they offered one thousand dollars, from the Wise Potato Chip Company, for information leading to the arrest and conviction of the murderer of Edward Fendt. This was done, says McKinley, about two and a half weeks after the crime was committed. Within a few days after that, three eyewitnesses came forward—Jennifer Knox, Clarissa Custis, and Jimmy Leland. All of them identified Darrell Mathes as the perpetrator and he was then arrested on November 17.

At this point, before Kellam begins his cross-examination, McKinley has been the state's most effective witness by far. Although his testimony was in no permanent way damaging to the defendant, he gave the impression of being a dedicated, capable, and experienced detective, one to whom you could entrust a murder probe with every expectation that *he* would find the killer if anyone could.

It is this impression—at least as it applies to the Potato Chip Murder Case—that Kellam is determined to destroy in his cross-examination. Destined to last for over four hostile hours, it begins with pleasantries and Kellam's broadest smile yet.

Kellam: "Good morning, Detective McKinley."

McKinley: "Good morning, Mr. Kellam."

Kellam: "And how are you today?"

McKinley: "I'm fine, Mr. Kellam. And how are you?"

The note of familiarity is to be sustained throughout the long day of testimony, but the note of affection vanishes soon after Kellam begins his questioning. He attacks with relish and gusto, as if he had been waiting for this witness all week. And McKinley appears increasingly vulnerable. He has no doubt sparred with Kellam many times before, but this appears to be of no advantage. His responses to Mendelow were crisp and confident. With Kellam he is hesitant, occasionally sheepish. To answer what seem to me to be simple questions, he must shuffle through a mass of notes and police reports, and even then he often speaks guardedly. By the end of the day, Kellam has introduced into evidence nineteen documents (exhibits "A" through "S"), and at least a dozen of them are presented to McKinley "to refresh your memory." (Kellam, too, has a good deal of coaching today. Occasionally in previous cross-examinations Singer had interrupted for brief whispered exchanges with his co-counsel. But today he is constantly leaping up from the defense table and, with his peculiar loping shuffle of a walk, crossing to Kellam to hand him notes and engage in intense conversations that we can almost, but not quite, hear.)

Within a few minutes Kellam has established that there were four other supposed eyewitnesses who gave information before the three teen-agers came forward. Two of the four, including the grocer to whom Fendt had just made the delivery, were named Harris. The third man was a Mr. Winifree. The fourth witness, the only woman, and, as McKinley admits, the most important in the initial judgment of the police, was a Clare Anderson. All four described the perpetrator as a black man in his late twenties, anywhere between five feet seven and six feet one in height. Two said he had a mustache, two said he was wearing a hat (one said white, the other blue), one said he had on checkered pants, another said plaid pants. The grocer Harris observed the man through his store window. The other Harris saw him on the street. Mr. Winifree was around the corner and claimed to have noticed someone hop into the parked black

Buick Riviera and drive away. Only Clare Anderson stated that she saw the perpetrator full face. She was standing on the sidewalk directly opposite the Wise truck: as the killer stepped from the truck on the passenger side, he looked her squarely in the eye before he turned and ran down the block. McKinley discloses this information grudgingly and it is even more painful for him to admit, under Kellam's probing, that he considered Clare Anderson's description of the suspect so reliable that it was used as the basis for a sketch drawn by a police artist. "And wasn't this picture later shown on the TV news?" asks Kellam. It was. "It was considered a good enough likeness of the man you were looking for, for you to give that picture to CBS News, to be shown on something they call 'Police Profile' and for the TV reporter, Chris Borgen, to give a description of the man on the air." Yes on all counts. Kellam then produces the sketch and hands it to McKinley for identification. It is entered into evidence. We are of course not permitted to see the drawing, but Kellam waves it around outrageously before Agresta commands him to put it down. I, and presumably most of the other jurors, see enough of the sketch to know that it looks nothing like Darrell Mathes.

Kellam turns from the four "other" eyewitnesses to introduce an entirely new line of questioning. After Jennifer, Clarissa, and Jimmy came forward, the police asked them to identify Darrell Mathes in certain photographs.

McKinley: "That is correct."

Kellam: "And where were these photographs taken?"

McKinley: "At Darrell Mathes's mother's funeral, I believe."

Kellam: "And when was that?"

McKinley (after checking his notes): "Friday, November 15, 1974."

So Darrell Mathes's mother died between the day of the murder and her son's arrest. The fact is startling in itself, but it pulses with implications for this trial. Will it increase sympathy for the defendant? Will his own story—if we ever hear it—reflect the circumstances of his mother's death? What does it do to the "image" of the police in this case to think of them, as McKinley describes them, lurking about the steps of the funeral home, trying to conceal their cameras, furtively shooting pictures of a bereaved family?

Two days after the funeral, on Sunday, November 17, McKinley testifies, Darrell Mathes was arrested, not at his home but in the Bronx, where he was staying with relatives. The police were led to him by his brother. "Aside from the pictures taken at the funeral home, did the police have any other way of identifying the defendant?" Kellam asks. McKinley uses this lead to telling effect. He answers, "There was nothing from his prior arrest—" Kellam, taken by surprise, interrupts angrily. He turns to Agresta, who decides that this is a good time to break for lunch.

I have lunch with Juror 6. After buying sandwiches at a deli across the street from the courthouse, we eat sitting on a bench in a triangular patch of greenery, smack in the middle of the flashing Queens Boulevard traffic. Luncheon on the grass, Kew Gardens style. For the first time, and quite discreetly, I mention the trial to a fellow juror. Our conversation is short and harmless: We both agree that Kellam is doing a terrific job and that the state seems so far to have no case at all.

Back in the courtroom, Kellam tries to extract the sting from McKinley's last disclosure. He gets the detective to explain that the defendant's prior arrest was handled by Family Court and thus neither fingerprints nor photographs were taken of Darrell at the time.

If the cross-examination is a duel, McKinley's sole hit is his revelation that the defendant was previously arrested. He is clearly pleased to have had the opportunity to get that out. Otherwise, his resistance to Kellam mounts as the questioning continues into the late afternoon. He is frustratingly precise, frequently answering questions "No, I didn't" when later the answer proves to be "Yes, the police did." This hairsplitting, however justified, leads to one glaring contradiction that Kellam, by persistence and force of lung power, finally wrenches from him.

Kellam: "At the time the kids came forward, how many suspects in the case did you have?"

McKinley: "I didn't have any."

Kellam: "You *didn't* have any."

McKinley: "No, sir."

Kellam: "You didn't have any suspects."

McKinley: "No, sir."

Kellam (eyes blazing): "Did you ever hear of a man named Simpkins?"

McKinley (after checking his notes): "Yes, sir."

Kellam: "And at that time, just before Darrell Mathes was arrested, wasn't this man Simpkins in the hospital with a bullet still lodged in his leg and wasn't he considered a suspect?"

McKinley: "By the police, yes, sir."

Kellam: "Did you ever hear of two men named 'Brain' and 'Savage'?"

McKinley (after checking his notes): "Yes, sir."

Kellam: "And another man named Worthy?"

McKinley (after checking his notes): "Yes, sir."

Kellam: "And didn't Mr. Worthy tell the police that street rumors had it that the potato chip man was murdered by 'Brain' and 'Savage'?"

McKinley: "Yes, sir."

Kellam (shouting now in a courtroom tight with tension): "And isn't it true that at the time Darrell Mathes was arrested the police had seven or eight suspects, that Simpkins and 'Brain' and 'Savage' were only three of them?"

McKinley (almost inaudibly): "Yes, sir."

Kellam relaxes—we all do, I expect—but just for a moment. He focuses now on the police line-up that was held the day Darrell Mathes was arrested. McKinley admits that Clare Anderson was brought to the line-up with Jennifer, Clarissa, and Jimmy, but she, unlike the kids, could not identify Darrell as the perpetrator. He admits further that neither of the Harrises nor Mr. Winifree was asked to come to the line-up; that, indeed, none of them was ever asked to identify the defendant as the person he saw running from the crime site. McKinley admits still further that a black Buick Riviera, stolen and abandoned, was impounded by the police and identified by Mr. Winifree as the car he thought the suspect drove away in—although, McKinley adds, checking his notes, "Mr. Winifree thought the car he saw was four-door and the car we found was two-door."* Kellam questions McKinley at length about the police investigation of the abandoned car until eventually McKinley confesses that *he* never believed the car was important to the case. He is never asked why.

In addition to the opening "And how are you today?" there are two other moments in McKinley's testimony that provoke smiles. At one point he explains that his investigation of the case was delayed for about two weeks while he attended a homicide seminar. Kellam greets this revelation with an exaggerated look that seems to ask: *"You* had to attend a homicide seminar?" which leads the detective to add, defensively, "I was ordered to go." I notice that Singer almost laughs at this.

Much more explosive is an outburst prompted by Kellam while questioning McKinley (rather briefly) about the kids' statements at the precinct house. The detective testifies that the interview with Jennifer was put on tape. Kellam asks if the other two kids were taped as well, and after checking his notes, McKinley replies that they were not. Without being asked why, he volunteers that personally he doesn't like to tape-record interviews. Kellam is at him like a shot: "Because they play back exactly what was said!" Mendelowe jumps to his feet to shout his objection. Agresta mildly asks that we disregard defense counsel's remark. The longest day of testimony is over at close to 4 P.M.

In the jury room and as we leave the courthouse, we are starting to disregard the judge's admonition not to discuss the case. There are no discussions in which we all join, but there are conversations involving two or three jurors, one of which I am part of, others of which I overhear. Juror 8 and the first (now

---

*Mr. Winifree's memory or perception *was* faulty. I have since learned that the Buick Riviera is available only in two-door models.

the only) alternate agree that Kellam made too much of Jennifer's testimony, as recounted by McKinley, as to where the other kids were standing when they saw Darrell Mathes, gun in hand. Was it the middle of the block or on the corner? Says one juror: "It don't make any difference where they were. They could still have seen the kid." Obviously they are missing the point Kellam was trying to establish: that Jennifer had contradicted herself in her two separate interviews with the police, first saying that the kids were on the corner, later that they were in the middle of the block. Presumably Kellam will hammer at these contradictions next week when the kids take the stand.

My own violation of the judge's rule was innocuous enough. Juror 6 and I agreed that at various moments we have had almost uncontrollable urges to shout out our own questions at the witnesses.

At around ten-thirty this morning the lights went out above Agresta's desk. They remained out for about ten minutes while one of the guards tinkered with the switch. Then they continued to flicker throughout the morning. Steady, sustained illumination is difficult to achieve in this courtroom.

PART THREE

The Kids

Ricky

RIKERS ISLAND is situated in the East River about twenty miles up from lower New York harbor, just beyond the bend where the waterway veers east toward Long Island Sound. The nearest "mainland," less than a mile away, is the bulge in the Queens coastline that is La Guardia Airport. It is so close that from any spot on the island you can look more or less to the southeast and see that modern symbol of flight, the terminal control tower. And throughout the day and night you can hear the roar of departing and arriving aircraft. Whether the planes are rising in takeoff or descending for landing, over Rikers Island their altitude is always low, their decibel count always high.

In the shadow, then, of a great center of travel and transportation sprawls an island whose only industry and whose only purpose is incarceration. Almost all of its many buildings provide housing for inmates, and those that do not are for the administration of those that do. Adult males (age twenty-one and over) live in a large cluster of squat, narrowly separated red-brick structures (the Men's House of Detention), females in a large concrete facility (the Women's House of Detention). Adolescent males (from sixteen to twenty) are confined to an enormous sweeping curve of a building, three stories high, which is the New York City Adolescent Reception Detention Center.

A relatively new facility—it was officially opened on June 17, 1973—the ARDC is described in its "Institutional Directory of Programs" as "a remand shelter . . . unique in the extent to which it provides opportunities and activities for the inmates in its custody. All inmates, no matter how short their stay here, will be able to engage in a variety of educational, social and psychological activities designed to aid them in their relationship with the environment from which they came and to which they will return." The pamphlet goes on to describe programs offered in high-school- and college-level studies, remedial reading, drug addiction treatment, Puerto Rican–Hispanic culture, theater and music, among several others. It lists medical, dental, and legal services available. It speaks of employment projects and welfare grants for inmates who are about to be released and of parole for those who are not. In all, the directory suggests an enlightened, progressive plan for dealing with adolescent offenders, a design for enhancing the capabilities, however modest, that an inmate has when he arrives so as to make him measurably stronger when he leaves. But somehow the reality of the ARDC is considerably different.

For it is, above all else, a place of detention, not merely of shelter, and evidence of its prime function is everywhere. From the gentle arc of the building radiate wings that are the various quads. Connecting the quads on each floor is a curved, pastel-colored cinder-block passageway, about a quarter of a mile in length from one end of the building to the other, interrupted from time to time by a baffling series of locked steel doors; along the passageways march groups of uniformed young men, over 90 percent of them black and Puerto Rican, in double file. They are on their way to or from classrooms or gym or mess hall or library or dayroom. No matter what, they are almost certainly either leaving or returning to their cells. These, whether they contain a single cot or bunk beds, are all of the same size and shape: six feet wide by eight feet long. Each is fitted with a toilet, a sink, a desk, one or two chairs, a small dresser. In place of bars the cells have slatted plastic windows looking outward, toward La Guardia Airport, and smaller plastic windows looking inward, onto the corridor separating the two rows of facing cells that make up each quad. The plastic of the windows is not easily broken, but here and there one sees evidence that it can be cracked and even penetrated if an object heavy enough is flung at it hard enough. It can also burn, and in cell after cell the windows in the doors are pitted with ugly amorphous holes where plastic has been melted away.

The holes are too small for anyone to crawl through, but if an inmate *were* to succeed in escaping through the door of his cell, he would find waiting for him at the interior end of the corridor a glass-enclosed control room manned by armed guards forever, if not conscientiously, on watch. And at the exterior end of the corridor he would find only a blank cinder-block wall. So if escapes are to be attempted, and they are, they must be made through the outside windows of the cells.

The weapons that might prove useful in an escape attempt are, surprisingly, more easily accessible than the means of exit. The architects of the ARDC building did not make allowance for the ingenuity and resourcefulness of its tenants. The false ceilings in the dayrooms and the corridors serve as perfect hiding places for knives and "rods" (strips of metal molding ripped from the walls and fashioned into weapons) and "brass knuckles" made from ashcan handles.

An attempted escape is but the most extreme manifestation of the craving for freedom that characterizes the inmates —and that one senses in the repressed energy of their bodies and the defiant glare of their eyes. The staff may at times see ingratitude in this craving, which is so prevalent and so persistent. After all, these young men are by and large neither abused nor ignored. Numbering somewhere between 1,000 and 1,100 (about 1,040 on the average while Ricky Mathes was among them), the youths of the ARDC are treated about as well as can be expected in a financially crippled city. A lack of funds has drastically reduced the innovative programs of which New York's Department of Correction boasted when the ARDC opened. At that time, 154 counselors were hired, but that number had been cut to 95 when Ricky was there. Today there are fourteen, and a spokesman for the Department of Correction says of the inmates, "We are not punishing them, nor deterring them or rehabilitating them. We are warehousing them."

As warehousing goes, the facility achieves at least passing grades. Certainly the inmates are more than adequately fed and sheltered and clothed. Given the relatively brief time served here—usually three to four months and, at least theoretically, never more than a year—the inmates have decent enough educational and recreational opportunities. They live in neither squalor nor danger. (Those who are judged to be potential psychopaths are segregated in a special quad under much tighter observation and security than is enforced elsewhere.) Indeed, there can be no question that many of these young men here enjoy a life of far greater comfort, safety, stability, and sustenance than they do in the slums from which they come. Nevertheless, says Ricky Mathes, in all the time he spent on Rikers Island, he did not meet a single inmate who did not want, desperately and fiercely, to get out.

He did not meet any inmates at all the night he arrived. It was past midnight, already Monday, November 18, and he was immediately isolated in a cell in the "segregation" quad, which is reserved for new inmates, for "old-timers" who are being punished for some violation of the rules, and for the psychologically disturbed. It is the last group that has given the segregation area the name by which it is more commonly known, the "bug-out."

Ricky was to remain there for about a month, alone in his cell and under careful and continuous scrutiny. He did not eat in the mess hall; meals were served to him and the other bug-out inmates in the dayroom at the end of the corridor. He did not attend classes, although twice a week he was permitted to use the gym. The reason behind the month-long segregation, Ricky explains now, is that "they think you're gonna do something funny." What "they" fear is more likely to be an attempt at suicide than an attempt at escape.

Ricky spent all of Monday, November 18, in confinement, but early the next morning he took the first of his many trips from Rikers Island to the Queens County Criminal Court Building. He was to see his attorney again, and this second meeting provided the first substantive opportunity for the two of them to get to know one another.

Stephen J. Singer, a graduate of the University of Vermont and Brooklyn Law School, was then thirty-one and had been practicing criminal law for seven years. Hard-driving and ambitious, but with a wide streak of idealism, Singer was then (and is now) registered with the 18B Panel of the New York State Administration of Legal Defense Panel Plan. This is the agency responsible for appointing lawyers to defend those who cannot afford private counsel. While many such cases are turned over to the Legal Aid Society, murder cases usually are not: Legal Aid attorneys are considered too inexperienced to handle them. Lawyers in private practice who register with the 18B Panel are called on a rotation basis as the need for them arises. When Darrell Mathes was arrested, it was Steve Singer's law firm that was due to be assigned to the next case. So that Tuesday morning, Singer drove from his home in the Bayside section of Queens, where he lives with his wife and two young sons, to his office in Kew Gardens, directly across the street from the Criminal Court Building; he had only to walk across Queens Boulevard, enter the courthouse, and find the "pen" (a cell in the courthouse) where his newest client was waiting for him.

The two had a relatively short time together (between fifteen minutes and a half hour) before they were due to appear before a judge. Singer remembers meeting "a frightened little kid," inarticulate, reticent, bewildered. How did Ricky see his attorney on that occasion? White, kind of short, not unfriendly, perhaps "businesslike" would be the best word. Singer's self-assurance—that air of confidence, skill, and practicality—made Ricky "a little less scared." Indeed, Singer's presumed capability was Ricky's only reason for hope; aside, that is, from his own claim of innocence.

It was this claim that he immediately urged upon Singer: "I didn't do it." But his alibi, in the lawyer's judgment, was virtually worthless. "Jurors rarely believe alibis that are dependent upon the testimony of family and friends," Singer explains. He was, however, pleased that Ricky had made no statements to the police. And if, on that day, he was inclined to believe in his client's innocence, it was at least in part because Ricky had no previous police record and because, curiously in a case of this kind, the arrest was made so long—more than a month—after the crime had been committed. With crimes involving robbery, such time lapses are rare: the police generally pick up a suspect soon if they are going to pick up anyone at all.

In the courtroom, Singer, with Ricky at his side, made a request for a preliminary hearing, also known as a felony examination—in which the state would be asked to present evidence to justify taking the case to the grand jury. But, Singer learned, it was too late for that: the case was already before the grand jury. Such a short-circuiting of procedure is not unusual in murder cases. When the district attorney's office believes it has found a killer, it will try to present its evidence to the grand jury as rapidly as possible.

It is also virtually a matter of policy for Queens judges to set no bail for murder suspects before they have been indicted. Thus, the hearing over and having achieved nothing, Ricky was returned by police bus to Rikers Island and the bug-out.

Steve Singer's records (and precise records they are, since court-appointed attorneys are compensated for their services only upon the submission of a time-itemized bill) show that altogether he was with Ricky for an hour and a half on the day of the second meeting, with most of that time spent in the courtroom. But however brief this introduction to the case was, it was sufficient to convince Singer that he had been assigned to a "ball-breaker." The matter of Ricky's innocence aside—and he was probably not yet persuaded to accept that—he believes that in general "the worst person to defend is a youth. . . . They have little respect for authority and they lie like hell. . . . I'm always skeptical. . . . They have to prove something to me. . . . At that time I doubted that [Ricky] was telling me everything."

To find out more, Singer was back in court with Ricky three days later. He presented a motion to appoint a private investigator to assist the defense in the preparation of its case. On November 26, the judge so ordered. By that time Ricky had been indicted on two counts of second-degree murder.

The grand jury had heard the state's evidence and handed

up its indictment—No. 4327/74: *The People* v. *Darrell R. Mathes*—on November 20, three days after Ricky's arrest. Neither Ricky nor his attorney was present during the grand jury hearing. By law they were barred from attending, for this was not an adversary proceeding.* It was merely the presentation by the Queens D.A.'s office of the People's case against Darrell Mathes. The grand jury in turn had merely to determine whether that case was strong enough to warrant the defendant's indictment and trial. What the grand jury said in effect was that there were sufficient grounds to impanel another jury eventually, one that would hear all the evidence, including the defense's attempt to weaken if not destroy the state's case, and make the final judgment as to Darrell Mathes's guilt or innocence.

Thanksgiving fell on November 28 in 1974, eight days after Ricky's indictment. For him the holiday was not only dreary in itself—a total contrast to the bustling, ubiquitous feast days he had enjoyed in the past—but also a cause of delay in the legalistic routine in which he was now trapped. The next step in that routine was his arraignment, scheduled for December 3, the Tuesday after Thanksgiving.

But on that day occurred the first, and the most preposterous, of the long, frustrating series of adjournments that was to plague the Darrell Mathes case for ten months and to keep Ricky on Rikers Island all that time. Correction officers brought the wrong person to court. It seemed that Ricky had a namesake in jail with him (although the two never met), and when Singer saw the stranger, he informed the judge that this was not his client. The case was then adjourned until December 5, when, it was hoped, the right defendant would be produced.

Two days later, Ricky himself was back in court. He was arraigned before Supreme Court Justice William C. Brennan, who set bail at the impossible sum of fifty thousand dollars. No one indulged in any thought, let alone talk, of Robert Mathes's being able to raise that amount of money.

*Ricky could have testified before the grand jury had he been willing to waive immunity, but he does not recall ever having been offered the opportunity to do so.

But if there was to be no freedom, there was at least fame of a sort. The next day the name "Darrell Mathes" appeared in the press for the first time. On October 15 the *Long Island Press*, a Queens daily, had featured the story of Edward Fendt's murder on the front page. (Illustrated with a photograph of the potato chip van, two policemen gazing out of its smashed front window, the report was as riddled with inaccuracies as Fendt's body was with bullets.) But Ricky's subsequent arrest and indictment went unnoticed. It was not until December 6 that the *Press* and the New York *Daily News* told their readers, in inside-page stories, that a sixteen-year-old St. Albans youth had been charged with killing the potato chip delivery man. Both papers gave Ricky's name, address, and bail amount correctly, but only the *Press* said, accurately, that he had been indicted the previous week. The *News* had both the grand jury indictment and the bail hearing happening the day before.

Singer's log shows that the hearing took all of half an hour, and, presumably, for only a small portion of that time was the lawyer alone with Ricky. All the same, Singer recalls that on that occasion he already noted a striking change in his client, a change that would be even more pronounced in the months to come. In a total turnabout, "Ricky," he says, "was developing into a tough guy, a wise-ass talking prison slang, fitting in with —and adjusting to—his new environment. A kid with no record was becoming one of the Rikers Island crew."

Today Singer's observation is met with a nod and a smile from his former client, and with one qualification. By the time of the bail hearing, Ricky had been in custody for almost three weeks, on Rikers Island for eighteen days. In what may well be a distinction without a difference—although clearly one that is significant to Ricky—he emphasizes that it was he who had changed himself rather than his surroundings that had changed him. He insists that he could not continue to be the quiet, frightened, vulnerable kid whom Singer first met and who was not the real Ricky anyway—not if he was to survive the long days and weeks and months of confinement.

And so, he now says, Rikers Island "was awright, with exceptions." He came to terms with it quickly and just as thoroughly he adopted its ways. But while he agrees that he soon was marching in lockstep with the other inmates, he also states flatly that in all the time he was there, he never once was guilty of serious misbehavior. For the most part, the authorities bear him out. "He was no trouble," says the assistant warden of the ARDC. But Ricky's file reveals that on three occasions he violated the rules.

He committed his first offense a couple of months after he arrived. No longer in segregation, he was nevertheless confined to a single-cell quad. In a cell adjacent to his was a boy named Tony. In a cell some distance away was Tony's friend, C.J. As one of the "crew," Ricky was quick to agree when,

> just before we was locked in, C.J. asked me if I would go to his cell so he could go into mine. He wanted to talk to Tony, who was next door to me, right? I was in C.J.'s cell for maybe two hours and then this CO [correction officer] walks by my cell and says, "Where's that little nigger that belongs in this cell?" So they found me, but nothin' much happened.

This infraction was followed by another that seems even less consequential. Says the assistant warden softly, almost sheepishly, his head bent to read the report, "He was found with contraband." He looks up and smiles. "A pair of sunglasses."

The violation here came to light because of Ricky's persistent attempts to assert his individuality in small gestures. If he heard a different drummer, the sound was faint, but one response to it was to decorate his cell in his own way. He was living in "Third Main of the Quad" then and with Billy, the second of his three roommates (Kendu was the first, Silky was the last). He recalls that upon being moved into Billy's cell,

> it didn't look too kosher to me. So when I came up there I had a lot of stuff to make the room look kosher . . . things that you buy in the canteen there. . . . We

fixed the cell up. We had pictures in frames on the desk
. . . mostly of my family and my girlfriends. We had the
room lookin' really, really nice. Everybody walked by
the cell and said, "Man, this dude just came up here and
hooked this room up." And the next day here come all
the CO's and ripped up the whole cell. This is called
"the shakedown." They come lookin' for razor blades or
somethin' ripped off—money or a ring or a watch or a
necklace. I was really upset. . . . I fixed the cell up again
. . . they bothered me some more. They come about . . .
once or twice a month. They really mess up a room.
Once they found some shades.

Ricky's third offense was by far the most serious. His file
reads that he was given "three days of punitive segregation for
destroying city property." What happened was:

A carton of cigarettes was missin' from my room. I knew
that the house gang [inmates whose job it is to change
the linens in the cells] took it. They had to be the ones.
So I started beatin' them up. Then the CO's came and
locked us all in the dayroom. I was mad. I started kickin'
the door real hard. They [the CO's] came to unlock the
door and I didn't see them comin'. So I'm kickin' the
door and then it swings back. Man, was there a crash!
But I didn't "destroy city property." Those doors are six
inches of steel. You can't do nothin' to them. But I did
get three days in the bug-out quad.

The new Ricky, he of the Rikers Island crew, was, then,
much the same as the old Ricky, whose fists would fly when he
thought he had been victimized or misjudged. But the new
Ricky was content to accept and to follow the regimen of the
ARDC:

You got up at six. You ate breakfast . . . finished about
seven, seven-thirty. Went back in [the cell] and got a
little lesson till nine. You're locked out [of the cell] at

nine, go to school, and come back at eleven-thirty. So when you walk in [the mess hall], they [the inmates who do not attend classes] will be eatin' lunch already. You're eatin' lunch and watch a little TV. Then you're locked back in. You're locked back out about twelve-thirty. Between twelve-thirty and two-thirty you're watchin' TV or studyin' or exercisin'. You could go to the gym only on a certain day at a certain time. . . . The whole quad went. In the afternoon you're locked back in at two-thirty and then you're locked back out at four for more TV or more studyin'. Then you're locked in till six. That's when you have dinner and you're locked out till nine-thirty. That's when they show you movies sometimes. Or you can watch some TV again or listen to the radio. At nine-thirty you're locked in for the whole night, until the next mornin' at six o'clock you start your whole day all over again, doin' the same thing.

Saturdays and Sundays were if anything even drearier. There were no classes, no movies, and no one was permitted to use the gym. There was nothing to do except watch TV. Visiting days for Ricky were not on weekends but on Tuesdays and Thursdays. His girlfriend Lala would visit occasionally, while his older sisters and brothers visited quite regularly; they, unlike their father, did not hold steady jobs.

The food was "eatable" and the classes were "good." During the two and a half hours of school every weekday morning he was taught the usual high school subjects—math, English, science, "all of 'em"—each by a separate teacher. And he learned more from them than he did from the teachers at Andrew Jackson. "The teachers [at Rikers Island] had time to suit and help everyone," he says revealingly, "and there wasn't anything else to do but study."

School records suggest a more troubled reality. Ricky was doing high-school-level work, admits the principal of P.S. 189 Annex (as the ARDC's academic program is officially known), but he was not a good student. Indeed, adds one of his teachers, who refuses to elaborate on the statement, "He was rebellious, disruptive, and hostile." The report of hostility comes as no surprise. Ricky's reply to the other charges is impassioned but weak.

> That teacher was always buggin' me. He was always
> comin' over to me to find out what I was doin'. I
> wanted to work in my own way. One time he come
> over to me and starts questionin' and I looked at him
> and told him to get away from me. . . . Then sometimes
> I wanted his attention and couldn't get it. So I called out
> in class. I had to, to get his attention, y'know. So he said
> I was disruptive.

In any case, according to the records, Ricky's Rikers Island schooling was as brief as it was undistinguished. For some reason, perhaps because of his frequent but irregular trips to court, he did not even start classes until May, almost six months after he arrived at the ARDC. Then school went into recess for the summer and when classes resumed in September, Ricky was in attendance for no more than a month.

He was markedly more successful in the only other organized activity in which he regularly participated, basketball. He and the six other inmates who composed his "building's" team played against "the other buildings," and won most of the time.

By far the preponderance of Ricky's "free time" was spent in watching television. With only two sets available to all the inmates in the quad, the choice of programs to be viewed was made by majority rule (as we shall see, such democracy breeds trouble). "Soul" was popular, as were sports programs and talk shows, but, surprisingly, most popular of all was the news. "Everybody wanted to know what happened out in the street. . . . 'Let's see what happened in Manhattan today.' Everybody was interested in what's happenin' out there in the borough where they lived."

For Ricky, and no doubt for most of the Rikers Island crew, "out there" was never very far from mind. However placidly he accepted it, Ricky always thought of the society of the quad as a temporary one. His permanent world was within him and none of the inmates or authorities were ever admitted into it. Lying in bed at night and listening to low-flying planes overhead, he would review in his mind the progress of his case, he would think of Lala and what was going on in the street, and he would try to imagine, over and over, why he was confined in this place. But he kept these important thoughts to himself and he claims that before he went to trial he never spoke to anyone about the reason he was in jail. "No one ever spoke over their case." And no one could have known that he was charged with murder—"not unless they went up to the control book and looked at the card."

He did, however, have some "good acquaintances"—his own roommates, Kendu, Billy, and Silky, a fellow named Rah and his roommate, Sherman. They were all older than Ricky— eighteen, nineteen, or twenty—and if he was not genuinely close to any of them, their companionship served to make the days tolerable.

The "exceptions" to the "awright" rating that Ricky awards to Rikers Island center for the most part on departures from the routine. The CO's were often young, twenty-three or twenty-four (of "mostly all kinds of races"), and therefore just barely older than the oldest inmates, of nineteen and twenty.

> And they [the CO's] want the young men to let
> themselves be hit by these officers. They expect the
> young men not to hit them back. That starts a whole lot
> of trouble. Some of the officers are awright, but some of
> them are not awright.

Other exceptions: "You don't get a doctor. You don't get enough walkin' around. You don't get enough gym." There was homosexuality, of which Ricky says with an uncharacteristic note of contempt, "I hate those homos." And, finally, there was "rioting"—actually sporadic bursts of violence between groups of inmates and CO's that raged "till someone got their head busted."

Steve Singer visited Ricky nine or ten times at Rikers Island; the news he brought was usually bad. The investigator's report, filed on December 23, was described by Singer, in a letter he wrote to Ricky the day after Christmas, as "not very favorable. You do not have an alibi for the date or time in question. Your alibi witnesses were of no value and could not confirm the time and date." The fact is that the investigator interviewed only one person who could have qualified as a potential alibi witness, Ricky's girlfriend Lala, then fourteen, and she refused outright the role offered to her. While she remembered being with Ricky at the park on October 14, she remembered little else. Her recall of time was exceptionally vague: she even thought Ricky's arrest had taken place two weeks earlier than it actually had.

Singer closed his letter to Ricky by asking, "If you have any idea as to who the youth might be who testified against you in the Grand Jury . . . , please let me know his name and address." At this point Singer had learned, by probing in the district attorney's office, that the state had at least one witness, male, who claimed that Ricky had confessed his guilt to him. But by the very next day Singer had heard "that the District Attorney's case seems to be based entirely on the testimony of two women." He then thought, however, that the "testimony was not to the effect that they witnessed a crime but rather . . . that the defendant told them on the date of the crime that he had committed it."

These tantalizing, clouded glimpses of the state's case were all Singer had at that time. He of course wanted much more, but a motion he had submitted, on December 16, to inspect the state's evidence had been adjourned to January 16. The material, he was told, was not yet available. On January 16 the motion was again adjourned, this time until February 3. On that date the motion was argued, but a decision was deferred until February 18. It was about then that the district attorney's office suggested some plea bargaining. Actually, such a thought had occurred to Steve Singer much earlier. On December 26, in a "memo for the file," he had written, "I must, unfortunately, suggest that we press the defendant for further information and perhaps even consider the possibility of plea discussion, regardless of his protestations of innocence." But although Singer certainly did press Ricky for further information—in vain, as it turned out—there is no written indication that he proposed plea bargaining to Ricky until prompted to do so by the district attorney's office.

At that point Ricky had been on Rikers Island for three months. He appeared in court each time a motion was to be argued. By letter and visits from Singer he was kept informed of the stumbling progress that was being made on his behalf. Certainly by the middle of February there was no reason for optimism. In effect, he had no alibi, and of the state's evidence against him his lawyer knew only that it was strong enough to persuade a grand jury to hand up an indictment. Thus, when the district attorney's office proposed, in exchange for a guilty plea, that the charge of two counts of second-degree murder be reduced to a "Class B" felony, Singer was obviously reluctant to dismiss the offer out of hand.

If found guilty of the original charges, Ricky faced a sentence of a minimum of fifteen years to life; the most he could get for a Class B felony was twenty-five years. Because of his age, he was not likely to draw a sentence anywhere near that long; in fact, it was safe to assume that, given good behavior, he would be free on parole within five years. Says Singer, "It wasn't a bad deal, but of course all I could do was to advise Ricky to think about it. I did think he was innocent, but I certainly couldn't be sure we'd win the case." Ricky, though, did not think about it. He refused to consider it for one moment.

In Singer's judgment, Ricky should not have had to arrive at a decision alone, and therefore, on February 24, he had Robert Mathes come to court to discuss the matter with his son. Ricky recalls that his father said very little. *He* apparently thought that the decision was Ricky's, and Ricky's alone, to make. In any case, says Ricky, neither his father nor Mr. Singer tried to influence him to change his mind. The original counts against him would stand and so would his plea of not guilty.

By February 27, a Singer petition to the court to reduce Ricky's bail had been denied, but the attorney had finally accomplished his initial objective: he had learned the identities of the state's star witnesses. Jennifer and Clarissa and Jimmy stepped from the shadows to dominate the case. And Singer went back to the Mathes house in St. Albans to check out whether there was "bad blood" between the families.

The first time he had visited there, he recalls, the atmosphere was almost hostile. "Not so much the father; he was always friendly. But in the beginning the brothers and sisters were tough . . . and cold. Y'know, a kind of 'What are you doing for my brother?' attack." He had come to seek out leads in the case, but had left with only resentment and irritation. The second visit was more cordial although even then Singer could sense lingering distrust. He came away knowing of the complaint sworn out against Joseph Mathes, in May of 1972, by Bessie Green, Jimmy Leland's mother.

Singer had sometime in December petitioned the court for an identification hearing on the case. Commonly referred to as a "Wade Hearing," this is a proceeding to determine whether photographs were taken or a line-up conducted in such a way as to taint the identification of the person later indicted for a crime. When he first made his request for the hearing, Singer knew virtually nothing of Jennifer, Clarissa, and Jimmy; he was simply trying to ascertain how reliable was the state's identification of Ricky as perpetrator.

While there was no reason to anticipate this at the time, the fact is that Singer's request for the hearing served to delay the start of Ricky's trial by many months. Of course, if the hearing had been successful for the defense—that is, if the court had approved Singer's motion to suppress the identification evidence—in all probability there would have been no trial at all. It did not work out that way.

The Wade Hearing was originally scheduled for March 18, before Judge Thomas S. Agresta, who had now been assigned to the case. The hearing was promptly adjourned in the first of a staggering series of postponements, a series that stretched from the end of winter until the brink of summer. The second adjournment was on April 7, because the district attorney's office was not yet ready. The hearing then began on April 14. Two witnesses were questioned: the police sergeant who had shown to the supposed eyewitnesses seven Polaroid snapshots taken at Livvie Mathes's funeral, and Detective William McKinley. The former testified that the kids had identified Ricky in five of the snapshots; the latter, that the kids had identified Ricky in the line-up. Singer made much of the facts that the snapshots, aside from being blurred, showed only one young man, Ricky, and that Ricky was without counsel at the time of the line-up.

It is wryly comic and terribly sad to read the conclusion of the transcript of the April 14 Wade Hearing. Singer, the district attorney, and the judge all seemed to agree that the proceeding would resume the following morning at nine-thirty, to hear additional witnesses. It actually resumed almost two months later. For that next day, April 15, the witnesses—the kids, of course—could not be found. Nor, in spite of subpoenas issued by the court, could they be found on May 5. Nor on June 2. On each of those dates the hearing had to be adjourned because of the absence of key witnesses.

When, finally, Clarissa Custis and Jimmy Leland were brought into court on June 3 (Jennifer Knox, presumably, still could not be located), they testified that they had identified Ricky in the snapshots and in the line-up. They also stated that they had seen Ricky leaning into and running from the potato chip truck while carrying a gun. When Singer tried to probe into this testimony, he was prevented from doing so by Agresta, who reminded him that the purpose of the hearing was solely to determine "whether or not the line-up or the photographs in any way tainted the in-court identification." His ruling at the conclusion of the proceeding was that they had not. Said Agresta:

> The testimony of the two individuals show [s] that they knew the defendant long before this incident occurred. . . . On the day of the incident they both identify the defendant as the person who approached a potato chip truck. . . . [They] had ample opportunity

to not only identify his face but his entire body. The court cannot find by any stretch of the imagination how this identification could have been tainted, suggested, or bolstered, by either the photographs or the line-up. The motion to suppress is denied. It's ridiculous.

Did Ricky, sitting in a courtroom for perhaps the fifteenth time since his arrest, think it was ridiculous? Perhaps, but he did not say so then and he does not say so now. A model of acceptance for all the court to see, he rose from the defense table and prepared to return to Rikers Island, there to wait out the long, slow summer.

What had Singer achieved? His client, still protesting his innocence as vehemently as ever, remained incarcerated, with no chance of release until the eventual conclusion of his trial. However, the attorney now knew two of the state's key witnesses and had an understanding of how they were likely to testify. He could study the transcript of the Wade Hearing and search for the flaws in their statements. He could ask Ricky about the occasion on which Clarissa said he visited her house. In addition, he now had copies of police reports that comprised a short history of the investigation of the crime. Laden with the names of a multitude of suspects, the "DD5"'s suggested various promising new leads. The case, in short, no longer looked so hopeless.

Unfortunately, he was soon to be in no position to act on his findings. During the month of June, Steve Singer was stricken with a serious illness, and on the thirtieth he formally requested of the court that he be relieved as defense counsel in *The People* v. *Darrell R. Mathes*. By early July he had entered the hospital for major surgery, and the court had assigned another attorney, Leroy B. Kellam, to the case.

Leroy Kellam is from Pinnacle, North Carolina, and Steve Singer is from Manhattan. On the surface, where color resides, they are as different as black is from white. Kellam seems big while Singer seems small. Kellam seems old while Singer seems young. Kellam seems hearty while Singer seems reserved. Kellam seems imaginative while Singer seems pragmatic. It is not difficult to conceive the surprise and the consolation—the sense of comfort, really—that Ricky Mathes must have felt when he first met his new defense counsel. Here was one of his own.

The grandson of a slave, Leroy Kellam attended West Virginia State College and began his career in New York as a bacteriologist, working first for the city's Department of Hospitals, then for the Department of Health. But at some point during the seventeen years he spent in laboratories, Kellam was drawn to the law and started studying at Brooklyn Law School at night. Fourteen years ago, at the age of forty-three, he began his practice. Today he is president of the Queens County Criminal Courts Bar Association and the Macon B. Allen Black Bar Association. His wife is a teacher of remedial reading at a Queens junior high school. His son, a senior in college, hopes to start law school next year. His older daughter works as a copywriter at one of New York's largest advertising agencies. His younger daughter teaches at a nursery school. The Kellams live in St. Albans, about twenty-five blocks from Ricky Mathes's house.

Of course Kellam is registered with the 18B Panel of the New York State Administration of Legal Defense. It was purely a rare instance of Ricky's good fortune that put Kellam next in line to be assigned a case when Steve Singer asked to be relieved.

Kellam says that he sensed Ricky's innocence within moments after he met him in the "pen" at Rikers Island. There is no question that Kellam has the keenest antennae when it comes to detecting racial injustice. But this was not simply a matter of suspected discrimination against a black. He says he saw Ricky's innocence in his eyes.

The problem was to bring it into the open, where everyone else could see it too. He reviewed the evidence that had been disclosed so far; he examined the documents; he talked to Ricky, he talked to the Mathes family. And he walked the streets of St. Albans.

Kellam's office, on Linden Boulevard, is only two and a half blocks from the Mathes house. Robert Mathes, while he says that he *always* believed his son would be found not guilty, took great heart from the coming of Kellam. "He did it. He did it by

walking the streets of this neighborhood," Robert Mathes maintains. He tends to disparage the white attorney's efforts: "It
didn't look good with Singer." But Ricky will always remind
him that "Mr. Singer did a lot for me, a lot." (And he believes
that Singer alone would have got him acquitted.)

On the street Kellam heard talk of "Brain" and "Savage"
and others who were suspected of having killed the potato chip
man. He ferreted out information about Jennifer and Clarissa
and Jimmy. He learned about the Mathes family and how Ricky
was thought to be the most promising of the older kids, the one
on whom his parents' highest hopes were riding.

That summer he tried to trace through many leads, but
none of them yielded a substantial new piece of evidence. He
was finally forced to acknowledge that in the courtroom his only
hope was to show how the police had been negligent in their
conduct of the investigation and how their key witnesses were
not to be believed.

On September 8 Steve Singer, out of the hospital and
recovered from surgery, asked the court to reassign him to the
Darrell Mathes case, at no fee for his further services. He made
this request, after receiving Kellam's approval to do so, not out
of a wild burst of nobility and idealism, but chiefly, he admits,
because he wanted to be part of a winning defense. The case
looked strong to him now; he would enjoy working with Kellam, whom he knew and respected enormously. And yes, he
believed that Ricky was innocent and deserved the most thorough defense effort he could get.

He and Kellam concurred immediately on how the work
was to be divided. They would alternate in interrogating the
batches of prospective jurors. Singer would make the opening
statement. Kellam would be responsible for all direct and cross
examination, although Singer would help him to frame the
questions and structure the attack. Kellam would deliver the
summation.

Kellam's late assignment to the defense had inevitably led
to further postponement of the trial. He needed time, the court
agreed, to familiarize himself with all the details of the case.
Furthermore, the district attorney's office was again having

trouble rounding up the state's key witnesses. And like everything else, the pace of the law is more leisurely in the summer-
time. By September 29 both sides had announced that they
were ready. *The People* v. *Darrell R. Mathes* was put on the
calendar. The trial—the selection of the jurors—would begin on
Thursday, October 9, 1975, just short of a year after the potato
chip man was murdered.

On Rikers Island that spring and summer, Ricky was faithfully kept informed of the delays and shrugged them off. He
claims to have felt no bitterness toward those responsible for
the postponements. And if he thought all the time, as he says
he did, of the injustice that kept him there, he spoke of it to no
one. He was content merely to get through the daily routine,
particularly since that routine was frequently jarred by the
unexpected and by explosions of violence. For Ricky, such incidents made Rikers Island "an interestin' place. . . . There was
always somethin' happenin'."

For one thing, there were constant fights—usually small
fights, not brawls—between black and Puerto Rican inmates.
The antagonism between these two groups was (and is) the most
severe security problem the ARDC faced. In the stiff and numb-
ing course of a Rikers Island day, hostility would erupt into
violence over the most minor disagreements: who was first in
the mess hall line, who was guilty of a foul in a basketball game.
Most frequently fights were caused by contention over radio
and television programs. The blacks did not want to listen to the
Puerto Ricans's preferred type of music and the latter disdained
"soul." (In June of 1976, a riot caused by some black inmates'
deprecating remarks about a Spanish-language television program left forty-one ARDC inmates injured and two hospital-
ized.)

Ricky, who admits that he does not like the way Puerto
Ricans talk, claims that he never got into any fights with the
"PR's" and was friendly with a few. Indeed, he recalls, one
Puerto Rican boy, named Freddie, actually became a hero: he
escaped.

Ricky heard of several attempted escapes during his time

at the ARDC, but none of the others was successful and none involved inmates he knew. He didn't know Freddie either—he was just "some Puerto Rican kid"—but Ricky learned (from a letter Freddie later sent to his former "associates") that the boy had managed to escape by crawling out of his cell window, jumping into the East River, and swimming to La Guardia Airport. Two other inmates had joined him, but they both had drowned.

And then there was the shower incident, which happened near the end. In every quad there is one large shower room, set among the cells. It is like any other shower room, in a country club, a college dorm, or a gymnasium, except that you are locked into it from the outside and it is graced with a large picture window facing out into the quad corridor. The fact that the person showering may thus be under constant surveillance is not necessarily a deterrent to horseplay. It certainly was not to Ricky, Silky, his roommate at the time, and another boy. They were in the shower for almost an hour, washing their bodies and their uniforms, and after a while they were having an uproarious time slapping each other with sopping-wet pieces of clothing. It was great fun until somehow the third boy managed to fall on the slippery floor and break his arm. The CO's, who had not been watching through the picture window, had to be called to take care of him.

By far the most memorable and chaotic incident was one in which Ricky himself supplied the precipitating force. "I had fights on Rikers Island," he confesses. The attack on the house gang for stealing his carton of cigarettes—though it indirectly landed him in the bug-out—was as nothing compared to the mess hall brawl. I need hardly say that Ricky describes this fracas with all the supercharged gusto and richly textured detail that he seems to reserve for his combat stories. Again he is telling me how he battled with his fists against what he considered wrong, and again he delights in every moment.

This particular fight began in the mess hall at breakfast time. Ricky had been sitting with three "brothers," who, when they were finished eating, seemed to ignore custom by leaving their plates on the table. As they started to walk away, Dave, an inmate on the mess hall crew, objected. Ricky continues:

> He told 'em, "You guys can't do this to me." You're supposed to take your trays and dump 'em. . . . So they got their plates. Bishme left a cup, his cup of coffee, on the table, just to be funny, right? So Dave picked the cup up and threw it on my tray while I was eatin' and said, "If you don't take it, I'm gonna beat you up." So I got up and I played Al Capone, pushed the table to the side, and we started fightin'. I saw him throw one and I threw about four, five times. . . . By the time I came to hit him the fifth time I seen this table flying to hit him in the face. I seen Silky comin' this way and Rah comin' this way and Eli comin' this way . . . chairs flyin' this way and this way and this way. . . . The riot squad walked in . . . and we chased them out of the mess hall, right out of the mess hall. We keep on fightin' till we're out of the mess hall too. But when we get out into the corridor the riot squad was out there with their sticks and helmets and bats and whatever else. . . .

Before too long the disturbance was brought under control and the inmates returned to the dorm. But that afternoon at lunchtime,

> everything [in the mess hall] looked funny because there wasn't as many CO's . . . there was only two CO's when there'd usually be eight, nine, or even ten. There was only one captain [of the mess hall crew] when there'd usually be three. . . . So they sat us in one hold. . . . Everybody was eatin'. . . . All of a sudden a garbage can flies by. Ooof! Turn around and all you see is people in white uniforms comin' with hatchets, sticks, butcher knives. . . . [It was the] fellers that work on the mess hall crew. . . . They was comin' against . . . the whole quad because we had come in there and beat up one of

these dudes that worked in the mess hall. Everybody
started scatterin' . . . and when we was gettin' to the
door, the CO's tried to close the door. It was a setup, of
course. . . . Everybody got out with a couple of scars on
their foot, couple on their arm. Then that night we
went back there and nothin' happened. They had a
different crew there workin'.

Dave, however, had not forgotten the beating he had suffered
and later that week he told Ricky, "It isn't over yet. I'm gonna
get you." A confrontation was arranged for the following Tuesday at sick call. It was to be *High Noon* on Rikers Island, but
Ricky, sophisticated in the ways of the ARDC, did not expect
a fair fight. Knowing that Dave would show up with his crew,
all in white mess hall uniforms, he took along a buddy and
defender named "Horse." A big guy, in height, width, thick-
ness, and intimidation, Horse announced to Dave, "Anybody
gonna jump in gotta see me. These old Don Juans y' all got ain't
gonna help you cuz I'm too big." It was, then, a one-on-one fight
after all, and there were no CO's around to stop it because the
inmates had locked the dayroom door. Says Ricky offhandedly,
"Me and Dave was fightin' and I beat him and sent him up. We
was already in sick call, so as soon as I beat him up he went to
see the nurse." So, however, did Ricky, who came out of the
fight with a "busted lip." But Dave's "nose was busted and he
had a black eye, couple of scars and scratches. So we ended
that."

The war between the mess hall crew and the quad continued in a state of uneasy truce for a long time. Ricky himself
was on the crew for four or five weeks, until he got fired for
"eatin' too slow." He explains:

I was gonna get fired anyway 'cause I had looked at
some papers in the office. The papers showed that the
mess hall crew that worked in the mornin' was supposed
to get paid thirty dollars a week. And we was only
gettin' paid fifteen dollars a week. When you work in

the mornin', you work in the breakfast shift and the
lunch shift. So they was gyppin' us, really. I got caught
by the CO lookin' at these papers. And the CO knew I
was goin' to tell the rest of the fellers who worked in
the mess hall. So he just found an easy way to shoot me
down. He shot me down for eatin' too slow. So I got
fired.

But to hear Ricky tell it, there was more action in the TV
room, which also served as a place for study, than in the mess
hall.

You'd turn the TV and get clobbered. There was a thing
in Sixth Main where all the brothers was lookin' at the
news and seein' what was happenin' in New York. And
somebody came into the TV [room] and turned to *I
Dream of Jeannie* or somethin', he got beat up. And if
you made any noise, ya got beat up because everywhere
in the corner somebody was studyin'. . . . And this one
kid got really beat up—this kid got slaughtered. . . . This
was when they had that plane crash right over in
Queens [of Eastern Airlines Flight 66 on June 24, 1975].
We was all lookin' at that and a kid got up and just
turned it—from the news, y'know. Some dude just
threw the whole TV at him. Aaaassshh! Man, he got *all*
beat up.

The studying that took place in the dayroom was serious
studying, according to Ricky, but not all of it was devoted to
subjects taught in class. There were some inmates who were
systematically planning the "jobs" they would pull after they
got back on the street. Among the more memorable:

There was one feller—this kid thought—I guess he still
thinks—that he could stick up—y'know that museum
with the big diamond in it? [The American Museum of
Natural History.] Yeah, that's the one. He's plannin' to

get that diamond. This kid do *nothing* but sit down and write and draw all day. He got pictures of it [the diamond], pictures of the museum, everything. He believes he's gonna get it when he's out.

During the spring and summer Ricky was studying and writing too—so conscientiously, he claims, that he earned for himself the nickname "Dr. Knowledge." But the reading he was doing was not entirely for school: at some point while he was on Rikers Island, if not before, he was drawn to the 5 Per Cent Nation, a black fraternal movement that, he explains, has as its goal "to bring about peace through wisdom and wisdom through knowledge . . . knowledge about science, ancestral history, mathematics, the earth." Ricky speaks of the 5 Per Cent Nation with uncharacteristic intensity. Its name, he says, stems from its underlying assumption that only 5 percent of the black people in the United States are prepared as individuals to make that leap toward wisdom or, in his words, "only someone in the 5 Per Cent is able to deal with himself within his own circumference to realize self-knowledge."

Ricky first learned of the movement even before he was arrested, from his brother Dwayne, but it was in the Rikers Island library that he discovered the basic texts. From these he copied, page after page after page, passages about the creation of the universe, its planets and its races; about sex and drugs and redemption; about the past and the future of the black man in white America.

In April, no doubt partly inspired by these writings and, to a notable extent, reflecting them, Ricky started to compose poetry. Before he left Rikers Island he wrote some fifteen "finished" poems and began but never completed countless others. All of them were written for his girlfriend Lala and the finished poems were mailed to her. But Ricky kept copies for himself and these were among his few treasured possessions. As such he carried them with him when, on October 9, 1975, after eleven months of incarceration, he boarded the police van to go to Queens County Criminal Court, to stand trial at last.

Doctor Knowledge Allah

"Dancing with Death"

I am dancing with life and death.
From the window I can see freedom.
Dancing with death.
I make love with freedom.
Dancing with death.
I can see my woman.
Dancing with death.
I am dancing with death in my cell.
I make love with death because I do not fear death.
I have moved from the living and deal with the dead.
Dancing with death.
I walk with death.
I speak with life.
If I had to ~~put~~ pick life or ~~the~~ death.
I would pick death.
Dancing with death.

Doctor Knowledge Allah

"Freedom and Nature"

My eye's is the window pain to my mind.
My eye's see freedom
The Nature of my woman is freedom.
I want to be free with my woman of nature.
Freedom and Nature.
I fit my mind to be free.
Thus my body is not.
Freedom and Nature
I can free my self from a mental death.
By dealing with Nature.
I can see my woman as the win blows.
She is very free to her self.
I am locked up but I am free.
Freedom is the mind.
Not the body.
Reality is beuatiful.
And beuaty is free.

Doctor Knowledge Allah

"America & Money"

America is the place of money
America is a land of hell.
Money bought my black people.
America sold them.
The white man bought them.
The white man paid them nothing.
Can the black man find their own Jewels.
America is a place of hell.
Like the devil have No heaven.
Can I find heaven.
If I seek or look for it.
Money is a vault of hell.
And the death of many people is money it self.
Even to go to court from Jail it takes money.

The Journal of a Juror

Monday, October 20, 1975

THE FIFTH DAY

THE WAIT in the jury room this morning seemed endless. For close to two hours we sat, patiently fidgeting, although a few of us used the time to advantage. Juror 5 read his book on horse racing; Juror 7 was well into the novel she began last week. Juror 3 was making impressive progress with her needlepoint. Juror 2 borrowed the second section of my *Times,* as he does almost every morning, to peruse the "Help Wanted" ads. When he returned it, Juror 6 borrowed it to study the stock market tables. I read the first section thoroughly.

But most of us, most of the time, simply talk. This morning there was chatter about what we had done over the weekend. The women seemed particularly interested in Juror 1's Saturday-night date, who took her to a Chinese restaurant (neither restaurant nor date was top flight). Our favorite topic since the trial began has been New York's fiscal crisis; this morning we were agitated by reports that some retired city employees were receiving more in pensions than they had made in salary. In any discussion of an "issue," one voice is usually a little louder, a little more confident, than any other—that of Juror 6. He is our resident expert on whatever the subject may be. There is no denying that, although English is not his native tongue, he is remarkably articulate. But he does go on.

We are finally ushered into the courtroom at eleven-forty, two hours after the last juror arrived. Agresta apologizes for the delay, promising to explain it when the trial is over. The first witness of the day is called, the first of the kids, Jimmy Leland, age fifteen. Mendelow speaks to him with gentleness, patience, and just a bit of apprehension. His questions tend to begin, "Now, Jimmy, try hard to remember . . ." and "Don't be nervous, Jimmy, but please try to speak up and tell the members of the jury . . ."

Jimmy testifies first that he lives with Lettie Lou Custis (mother of Jennifer and Clarissa), whom he calls "Mother"— even though some of the time he stays with his real mother. She is known variously as Bessie Green and Helen Himes (sp?)—he is unable to spell the latter name for the court reporter—and she owns and lives above a Linden Boulevard laundromat. Jimmy's answers are as brief and thin as drops from a leaky faucet. He speaks as if it were painful for him to do so, slurring his words and mumbling so softly that several times other jurors and I have to ask that he repeat his statements.

He testifies that on October 14 at 5 P.M. he was riding in a car with Mrs. Custis, Jennifer, and Clarissa. The car had an accident (it hit a parked car) and he and the other two kids got out (he first, followed by Jennifer and then Clarissa). He walked toward a corner food shop, saw someone "half in, half out" of a parked potato chip truck, changed his mind about going into the food shop, turned back toward the Custis car, heard the sound of glass breaking, turned around, and saw someone run from the truck and past where he was standing. The person was carrying a gun in his right hand, a .38.

Mendelow: "Is the person you saw here in the courtroom?"
Jimmy: "Yeah."
Mendelow: "Will you show us, please, Jimmy, who that person is." (Jimmy points to Ricky Mathes.) "Let the record show that the witness pointed to the defendant. I have no further questions."

As he did with the police witnesses, Kellam begins his cross-examination rather deferentially. He quickly establishes that Jimmy knew Ricky from the neighborhood, had once given him a cigarette (in his mother's laundromat? it's not clear), and that Ricky's older brother had once been arrested on a complaint sworn out by Jimmy's real mother. But Jimmy doesn't know what caused the trouble between them. He recognized that Ricky's gun was a .38 because he himself had once had one, *at the age of eleven,* but, he says, he "threw it away" the day after he got it. He describes Ricky's clothing as burgundy pants and burgundy shirt, no hat, and claims he knew nothing of the reward that Wise offered until this morning, when his mother, who presumably accompanied him to court, told him about it. Although he says he did not discuss what he had seen with Clarissa and Jennifer, only with the police and an assistant district attorney, he admits that he frequents a delicatessen where, we know from McKinley's testimony, a reward notice was posted.

Court recesses for lunch at one o'clock, reconvenes at about two-thirty, with Jimmy still on the stand. Jennifer Knox is called at about three. She's obviously "street smart," tough, self-assured. She's also about six months pregnant, at the age of eighteen. She says she's been in Amarillo, Texas, for the last two months, finishing high school there at a school for "unwed pregnant ladies," and living with the father of her unborn child, a man named Arthur Catledge, whom she has known for about three years.

In response to Mendelow's questions, she testifies that she saw Ricky at about 4 P.M. on October 14, when she was going to the cleaners; he was with two other boys whom she didn't know and who walked on when she approached. Says Ricky told her that he was going to rob the potato chip man and asked her if she wanted to join him. She said no. (This conversation, she later testifies, lasted ten minutes.) Then at 5 P.M. she was riding in a car with her mother, her sister, Jimmy, and her mother's boyfriend Jesse, and they had an accident. She says she and Clarissa left the car and walked to the grocery store, where they bought a loaf of bread. Then she started back to the car, got to the middle of the block—with Clarissa about five feet ahead of her—heard two shots, and saw Ricky running away from the potato chip truck, with a gun in his hand ("little and brownish"). She stopped him and asked what he was doing. He said he'd just shot the potato chip man. She asked him why and he answered that he wouldn't give him his money. Then he ran on toward the corner.

Under cross-examination, the most striking inconsistency revealed is the fact that at the grand jury hearing Jennifer testified that she was *"on the corner"* when she saw Ricky running away. This portion of the transcript is read to her by Kellam, but with absolute cool and not even an attempt to explain the discrepancy, she again maintains that she was standing in the middle of the block when she saw Ricky.

She also discloses that Ricky had visited her mother's apartment on two occasions: first at a party, where Ricky broke the arm of a chair and was asked to leave, and then a second time, not elaborated upon.

She says that Ricky was wearing "burgundy double-knit polyester pants," a "leather" (jacket, she explains to the judge), and white Pro-Keds. He was not wearing a hat. Like Jimmy, she claims she knew nothing about the reward until this morning, when Detective McKinley told her about it. On redirect examination, Mendelow brings out that two detectives had to visit Amarillo to get her to return to testify.

To Kellam, Jennifer is blatantly hostile and insolent, at times daringly defiant. At one point, a dramatic moment, she turns to Agresta and accuses Kellam of trying to confuse her, but, says she, she won't let him. In the face of her contradictory statement at the grand jury hearing about where she was standing when she saw the defendant running away, she is almost smug in now insisting that she was in the middle of the block. She assumes an air of superiority when she explains that while she may have been in stores where the reward announcement was posted, she never bothers to read things like that.

At one point Mendelow seems about to ask her why she

waited so long to go to the police, but he no sooner asks the word "why" when Kellam objects and the objection is sustained. (For me the biggest double mystery of the day: why *did* she wait and why wasn't Mendelow permitted to ask her the reason?) Agresta picks up the questioning and ascertains merely that she was living in New York and in the same neighborhood —though not necessarily with Mrs. Custis—for the month or so following the crime. Another unlikelihood, in terms of ordinary human behavior: again like Jimmy, she claims that she told *only her mother* about what she had seen. The three kids supposedly did not discuss the case even in the car when they were first driving to the police precinct, where they were then questioned separately.

Jennifer is dismissed at four forty-five and the court is recessed immediately after. During a brief break in the afternoon, jurors complain that it's so difficult to follow testimony regarding where witnesses were standing without being able to see the diagrams and photos. We have to remember that on a diagram Kellam entered into evidence Jimmy noted his movements in a dotted ink line, while Jennifer indicated where she was standing with an "X." At times it seems witnesses say 200th Street when they mean 202nd Street or 201st Street, and it's certainly not at all clear which stores they are constantly referring to.

Contradictions and improbabilities infest today's testimony like maggots in rotting meat:

1. Jimmy said Ricky was wearing a burgundy shirt; Jennifer said a leather jacket.

2. Jimmy said he was the first one to leave the car; Jennifer said she wasn't sure if he ever left the car—so obviously she left before he did.

3. While Jennifer said several times that she had just left the *grocery store* when she saw Ricky with the gun, at one key moment she said the *cleaners.*

4. Jennifer said that Clarissa continued walking ahead of her when she, Jennifer, stopped to talk to the fleeing Ricky, but

she then placed Clarissa no more than five to ten feet ahead when her conversation was over. Clarissa would have been much farther ahead than that if Jennifer had stopped to have a conversation, however brief.

5. It's hard to believe that Jimmy changed his mind about getting something to eat—"wasn't hungry anymore"—just before he got to the food store.

6. It's hard to believe that neither Jimmy nor Jennifer heard about or read the reward notices.

7. It's hard to believe that the three did not talk about the crime among themselves.

8. It's hard to believe that Ricky would have told Jennifer of his plan to rob the potato chip man and harder to believe that he would have invited her to join him. Depending on which aspect of Jennifer's testimony is emphasized, either they hardly knew one another or there was bad feeling between them (broken-chair incident).

9. It's hard to believe that Ricky would know at 4 P.M. that he would have the opportunity to rob the potato chip man at five.

10. The most glaring inconsistency: Jennifer's testimony as to where she was standing when she saw Ricky running away —first at the corner and then in the middle of the block.

Tuesday, October 21, 1975

THE SIXTH DAY

We have to wait until ten-fifty before being brought into the courtroom, simply to be told that today's witness had not yet arrived. Agresta wants to give her another hour and then, if she does not show up, he will dismiss us. Back in the jury room, Juror 7 breaks out a deck of cards and a penny-ante poker game begins—players include Juror 7, a woman, and four others, all men. Shortly after twelve, we are herded back into the courtroom, to be dismissed for the day and to be given the following timetable by Agresta: "We should wrap this up by tomorrow night and I should be able to give you the case on Thursday."

On the way home, Juror 10 remarks, "I think it's going to take a long time for us to come to a verdict." When I ask whether her opinion is based on intuition or what she has observed, she answers, with a slightly embarrassed smile, "Just from what I've heard." I've noticed that four of the women jurors—but not Juror 7—have been going to lunch together every day. Apparently they have not resisted the temptation to talk about the case—and who can blame them?

Wednesday, October 22, 1975

THE SEVENTH DAY

Court convened shortly before noon for what was to prove to be the final day of testimony. By the end of the day I was to feel emotionally drained and for the first time I was to regret my eagerness to serve on this jury and my having been selected for it. Tomorrow, I'm afraid, could become a nightmare.

The witness who did not turn up yesterday, Clarissa Custis, was called to the stand at noon. She is fifteen, soft-spoken, and though both fearful and defiant, much more appealing than either her tough older half-sister Jennifer or her dull "brother" Jimmy. Mendelow addresses her even more tenderly than he did the other two. When asked what she remembers of October 14, she starts her reconstruction before 4 P.M., when she and Jennifer went to the cleaners. (Presumably this was the occasion for Jennifer's meeting and talk with Ricky, but Clarissa makes no mention of such an occurrence, though she does offer a seemingly irrelevant detail that Jennifer omitted: When they got back from the cleaners, they went out again, for bread, but before they got to the store their mother drove by in her car, honked the horn at them, and they got in and drove home with her, but of course without the bread. At some later point (when? not mentioned in direct examination) they all (Clarissa, Jennifer, Jimmy, Mrs. Custis, and her boyfriend) got back in the car and drove to Murdock Avenue, where the car accident occurred. Clarissa says that she and Jennifer then got out of the car and walked to the store. She adds another new detail: she went into one part of the store to buy candy and Jennifer went into another part of the store to buy bread. They left by separate exits, Clarissa first, and apparently it was while she was waiting for Jennifer that she saw Ricky leaning ("half his body in the truck, half his body out") into the van, with one arm extended. She then heard two shots. By this time Jennifer had come out of the store and they started to walk to the corner, again Clarissa in front. (She would have us believe—and perhaps some of us will—that the sound of shots firing did not make the girls stop.) Another detail introduced now: they had a conversation as they walked—or at least they exchanged some words about the candy Clarissa had bought. Jennifer asked for some and Clarissa gave it to her, handing it to her behind her (Clarissa's) back, because they were walking single file. By this time they had progressed beyond the stores, apparently were close to the corner of 202nd Street, and Ricky came running by. He talked to Jennifer—Clarissa couldn't hear what he was saying—and then ran on. Clarissa asked Jennifer what he had said. She told her, "He said he shot the potato chip man because he wouldn't give him his money."

Some of the above was ascertained under cross-examination, particularly the testimony about the candy and how far up the block the two girls had walked when Ricky ran past them. Again Kellam was trying to stress the conflicting statements about where these kids were when they saw Ricky. Could he have torn other holes in Clarissa's story? We'll never know.

Clarissa has been on the stand for almost an hour when Kellam starts on his next line of attack. He asks whether Jimmy was with the sisters when they observed the defendant running from the potato chip truck. Clarissa replies that he was not. Kellam registers great surprise, then frowns, and starts to read from a document Singer has just handed to him. It is a statement Clarissa made to an assistant district attorney (not Mendelow) on November 14, 1974. As soon as he reaches the end of a passage that has Clarissa saying she was with Jennifer *and Jimmy* when she saw Ricky run past, Mendelow is on his feet, demanding to know whether the document from which Kellam has been reading has been properly identified and entered into evidence. There follows some judge-and-lawyer talk (a "sidebar," I believe it is called), out of hearing of the jury. On the witness stand, Clarissa's fingers are busy. She is squirming. Suddenly, her face contorted with pain, she looks up to the judge and says hoarsely, "I think I'm going to vomit." She clutches her throat. Agresta asks, "Do you feel sick?" Clarissa nods. The clerk of the court springs into action, rushing Clarissa out of the witness box and into a seat in the spectator area. She does not let go of her throat until she is seated. The eyes of everyone in the courtroom are upon her. Clearly agitated, indeed to the point of exasperation, Agresta declares a recess until two-thirty. It is 1 P.M.

As we assemble to be led to the elevator, several of the jurors express sympathy for Clarissa under the barrage of Kellam's questions. Says Juror 4, "The poor kid really looked sick even before she spoke to the judge. Why did Kellam have to badger her like that?"

Between two-thirty and three o'clock there's poker in the jury room again, with the same players. Juror 7 is doing very well, I'm told. Once we are in the courtroom, the judge makes a startling announcement: This morning's witness is too sick to continue on the stand. Agresta immediately adds that we must take the court's word for this, that we must not allow her failure to resume testifying to influence us in the slightest. He goes on: Because she can no longer appear and in order not to delay the trial again, prosecution and defense have agreed to play for us a tape recording of an assistant district attorney's interview with Clarissa on November 14, 1974. The court reporter grumbles about this, saying that he's not sure he can take this all down for the record, and in the day's only light moment, Agresta assures him that he can. ("And if you can't, I can take it down myself—in longhand.")

It is a little difficult to understand every word spoken on the tape, but Clarissa's statement is audible and distinct in all important details. There are three major inconsistencies—either with her own testimony in court or with that of the other kids: first, where she was standing—the tape clearly says on the corner; second, whether Jimmy was with her and Jennifer—the tape reveals that in November, 1974, she said he was; and third, the time she left the car—on the tape she clearly said five-thirty. With the conclusion of the tape recording, the state rests.

Kellam, as he begins the case for the defense, surprises at least two jurors. He calls as his first (and, it turns out, only) witness Darrell Mathes. The defendant is very thin, as I had observed all week, about five feet ten, walks with a springy, strutting step. He speaks up and, given the circumstances, does not appear overly tense. But he never looks at the person addressing him—not even Kellam. His eyes dart around the courtroom and never find a place to rest. As he testifies, I feel a compulsive need to *know* whether he's speaking the truth, or lying, with every statement he makes. If only it were possible to penetrate his brain—and the brains of the others, for that matter.

With Ricky on the stand, Kellam's approach changes dramatically. Gone is the jocularity, the condescension, the suspicion, and the hostility with which he treated the various prosecution witnesses. To his own client he is gentle and quiet and grave.

At Kellam's prompting, Ricky tells us that he is seventeen and until last year attended Andrew Jackson High School. The clear implication is that he has not been in school since November 17, 1974, when he was "picked up"—his words. I assume this means that he has been in jail since then, not out on bail. Ricky doesn't really remember very well what he was doing on October 14, 1974. He doesn't have a watch. Sometime in the afternoon he went to Cambria Heights Park to shoot baskets with some kids. Then he sat on a bench for a while and talked to his girlfriend Louella Johnson. He was in the park for about two hours and then went home. He had dinner with his mother about five-thirty. October 14 was a holiday, but the next day he went back to school and he continued to go until he was picked up. He first found out about the crime when he read the reward notice in the deli.

Kellam asks him about his previous arrest, mentioned by McKinley last Friday. Ricky says that it happened about three years ago in Brooklyn, where he was visiting his aunt. He and his cousin were picked up for "busting a hole in a factory window." They were taken to the police station, but were released when the police dropped the charges. Ricky says he has never held a gun in his hand.

Kellam asks Ricky about Clarissa and Jennifer and Jimmy. He says he knows them, has visited their house at least once, but is not really sure how many times; was aware that Jimmy's real mother had had his brother arrested. But he insists he was on good terms with them and does not know why they would tell these lies about him.

Concluding his direct examination, Kellam asks Ricky, emphasizing that he is "under oath," whether he killed the potato chip man. Ricky, with every bit of earnestness he can muster, replies, "No, sir."

Mendelow now assumes a rare posture. For the first time he is on the offensive, and he quickly gets Ricky to admit two extremely damaging facts. (So it didn't take long to realize the danger to the defendant in taking the stand in his own defense. Would he have been better off not testifying? Perhaps I'll know tomorrow.) First, although Ricky claims he was in the park in the earlier part of the afternoon, shooting baskets, he cannot name a single boy who was playing with him—not one. Obviously, then, none of them are in the courtroom and none of them will testify for him. Undermining his credibility even more is the fact that his girlfriend (Louella Johnson), whom he claims to have talked with in the park *after* he played basketball, is also not present in the courtroom and will not testify. Less damaging, but curious: Ricky later "remembers" under cross-examination that he left the park around four-ten. There's quite a bit of by-play between him and Mendelow about his first statement that he did not remember exactly when he left the park and his later recollection that it was about four-ten: Ricky insists that there's no contradiction here because not remembering exactly and then saying *around* four-ten add up to the same thing. At this point, a woman in the spectator section shouts, "Right on, Ricky!" Her cry is like an explosion in the courtroom. (Today, for the first time, Ricky has a "cheering section" of about fifteen to twenty people. The group includes a man who must be his father; he was in and out of the courtroom last week, but has attended regularly since the three kids began their testimony on Monday.) Kellam whirls around and, with a furious shake of his head, admonishes the woman who cracked our decorum.

To me the significance of four-ten is negligible. Under no circumstances could the kids he claims to have played basketball with or Louella Johnson have provided him with a conclusive alibi. He could easily have been with them in Cambria Heights Park at four-ten or four-twenty or even four-thirty and still have been at Murdock Avenue and 201st Street by five. However, the fact that he can get none of these kids to appear for him does suggest that the whole park story may well be false.

After casting heavy suspicion on the key element of Ricky's testimony, Mendelow tries to establish how familiar Ricky is with the Murdock Avenue shopping area where the crime took place. He claims not to know the area at all. Mendelow: "You've lived in the neighborhood for ten years and you've never gone shopping on Murdock Avenue?" Ricky (bitingly): "I don't go shopping!" Mendelow finally forces Ricky to admit that he does frequent a candy store on 198th Street and Murdock Avenue. Ricky: "Buying candy is not shopping." And 198th Street is not 201st Street.

Mendelow then brings up the Brooklyn incident that led to Ricky's first arrest. He asks the name of the aunt he was visiting at the time. Ricky tells him, but then, when asked her address, he says he doesn't know. Mendelow makes much of this and both voices rise, Mendelow's accusingly, Ricky's in anger (but I consider the whole line of questioning totally irrelevant—the incident took place about three years ago). Mendelow: "How could you visit your aunt without knowing where she lives?" Ricky: "Because I went with my mother!"*

Mendelow zeros in on the fact that Ricky remembers precisely the time he had dinner on the night of October 14 when he doesn't remember the precise time of anything else. Ricky explains, patiently, contemptuously, that there is a clock on the kitchen wall and he looked at it when he walked in for dinner. When asked what time he had dinner on various other nights —and Mendelow barks out dates chosen seemingly at random —Ricky keeps repeating, his voice rising almost to the edge of fury, "I don't remember!" Then, as if administering a *coup de grace* to a vainglorious and despised opponent, he shouts out what clearly he considers a triumphant disclosure: "Some nights I don't even have dinner! I just eat a ham sandwich!"

Mendelow subsides. He speaks almost softly as he addresses his final question to Ricky: "Now, Darrell, are you claiming, *under oath,* that Clarissa and Jimmy and Jennifer all lied when *they* were under oath?" Ricky answers, "Yes" (no "sir"—that was reserved for his lawyer). Mendelow has no further questions.

In redirect examination, Kellam establishes that Ricky lives closer to another shopping area, on Linden Boulevard, than to the Murdock Avenue stores, which are five or six blocks away. Kellam then asks how Ricky happens to remember so well having dinner with his mother on the evening of October 14. Ricky says, "Because she told me a lot of things that night— things that she wanted me to start doing and stuff like that." Kellam: "She was sick then?" Ricky: "Yes." Kellam: "What things did she say to you?" Before Ricky can answer, Mendelow

*At home tonight as a test I asked Jared his aunts' street addresses. For Judy he said 49 Montgomery Street (correct answer: 29 Monterey Drive). For Renée he said Paine Avenue (correct, but he did not know the number). For Ruth he had no idea at all. But what would it have proved if Ricky did know his aunt's address?

objects on the basis of hearsay and the objection is sustained. The defense rests. There will be no more witnesses.

Our knowing that Ricky's mother was dead within a month after October 14 gives the last bit of testimony a poignancy uncommon in this trial so far. I for one am eager to know what Ricky's mother said to him that evening. The entire spectacle of Ricky fighting for his life—well, certainly his freedom—had a chilling impact on me. That the fabric of his testimony may have been patched with lies—particularly that earnest plea of innocence—is a possibility I am always aware of. But his youth and the possibility that he was not lying and the fierce instinct of self-preservation he displayed left me shaking.

Just remembered another line of Mendelow's questioning: Ricky's schooling. He said he was doing "all right." Without being completely direct about the matter, he gave the clear impression that his grades were mediocre at best. If he had claimed otherwise, I'm sure Mendelow had the evidence to prove he was lying. The prosecutor then turned to Ricky's attendance record and forced him to confess that he had never attended music ("I don't need music," he shouted) and had frequently cut science. He maintained that he did attend all his other classes regularly, and since Mendelow did not pursue this, presumably he was telling the truth.

Hours earlier—when none of us had yet known that Clarissa would not resume her testimony and that Ricky would be the first and last witness for the defense—at least four of us had willfully and shamelessly disregarded the court's instructions and discussed the case at length. We were at lunch, at the kosher delicatessen across the street from the courthouse, and the conversation began almost as soon as we were seated. It was sparked, I'm sure, by Clarissa's sudden and shocking departure from the stand. I can't recall which one of us broached the matter—it was not I—but I certainly did nothing to discourage the talk. On the contrary, I was pleased to have this opportunity to detect how the wind was blowing. It was pretty obvious that Jurors 4, 5, and 6 are leaning—perhaps an understatement—toward a guilty verdict. There was much commiseration with the three kids because of Kellam's brutal attempts to confuse them and demolish their stories. Said Juror 5 (on in years but not in wisdom): "Christ, it was like *they* had committed a crime." (Plainly he's oblivious to the fact that if they did not speak the truth while on the witness stand, they did commit a crime—perjury.) Said Juror 4 (middle-aged, mild-mannered, decent, one of the most likable of the jurors): "There's nothing wrong if the kids didn't come forward until after the reward was announced. That's what the reward was for." When I asked if the three thought Ricky would testify in his own defense, Jurors 4 and 5 both said no. (Juror 5: "It will make what's bad even worse.") But Juror 6, who had been surprisingly silent through most of the conversation, said, most ominously of all, "He'd better."

As we were walking from the courthouse at the end of the day, Juror 5 asked why the girlfriend didn't testify and give "him" an alibi. Juror 8, after looking around to see who, if anyone, was behind him, imitated the way those "young punks" walk. It was a perfect imitation of how Ricky had strolled to and from the witness stand.

Ricky may be guilty. I'm sure I will never know. But I find the testimony of those three kids so full of contradictions, inconsistencies, gross improbabilities—things I just cannot attribute to failure of perception and memory—that the state's case sinks like a torpedoed boat. Ricky's guilt has certainly not been proved beyond a reasonable doubt. Indeed, in the face of evidence like this, it's farcical to use the word "proved" at all. However, I dread both having to try to persuade others to go along with my view and even more the prospect of being the lone holdout against eleven others. But if I have to "hang the jury," I will.

PART FOUR

The Jury

Ricky

EVERY MORNING during the trial, when Ricky Mathes left Rikers Island he carried with him the possessions he valued most, his pictures and his writings, because every day there loomed the possibility that he would not have to return. He had no hard grasp of the legal developments that could bring this unlikely event to pass. But as long as there was even a chance that before nightfall he would be free, he did not want to have to go back just to retrieve his treasures.

Among those treasures he certainly did not include his clothes. As an inmate he dressed in an ARDC uniform, and the clothes he had worn on the day of his arrest he had long since outgrown. Police records show that he stood five feet nine inches tall on November 17, 1974. By October, 1975, he had edged beyond six feet. And his weight was of course greater than it had been a year ago, although probably not by very much.

So the clothing Ricky was to wear during the trial presented a problem. Robert Mathes did the best he could, bringing shirts and trousers to Rikers Island from home, but none of them fit his son very well. And Ricky, who exults in his passion for clothes, was a good deal less than a model of fashionable tailoring throughout his ten days in court.

He reached the Queens County Criminal Court Building by 8 A.M. each morning. Until the trial began for the day, and during all recesses, he would wait in a holding area of the court called the "bullpen." It was actually a cell a few steps from the courtroom. The cell would be crowded in the mornings, when several defendants were brought to court for hearings, but by afternoon only those who were actually on trial, no more than one or two, would still be there. Ricky passed the time by talking with some of the other defendants and by writing poems and reading. On the first Thursday, when, the original Juror 8 not having shown up, the trial did not resume until early afternoon, Ricky, for the first time in his life, started and finished an entire book in one day. "I read 160 pages," he says proudly. The book was *The Night of January 16th*, a novel by Ayn Rand, of all people, and Ricky had borrowed it from the Rikers Island library. It's the story of a trial, "a nice book," says Ricky, and sitting in his cell, he enjoyed it more than any book he had ever had to read for school.

He ate his meals alone in another cell, on a lower floor of the courthouse. In addition to lunch, he was given a seven-o'clock sandwich snack every evening because, regardless of when his trial adjourned for the day, he would never leave for Rikers Island before eight or nine, when the police bus came to pick him up. It would then be close to ten o'clock before he got back to the ARDC. There, in another holding area, or bullpen, he would be served dinner and would wait around again. It was eleven or later, he says, when he was finally brought to his cell and locked in for the night. Since Silky, his roommate at that time, would be asleep by then, there was no one Ricky could speak to about the day's court developments, even if he had been inclined to do so.

In general, he thought those developments were encouraging, at least until the final evening. During the early days, when the jury was being chosen, he may have sat at the defense table slumped and immobile, but, he assures me, he was keenly interested in what was happening. Indeed, when I ask if he was paying attention to the selection of the jurors, he answers, "I was payin' *a lot* of attention to the jurors, *period.*" Those shifting eyes that never seemed to light on anyone for very long he explains as a kind of optical trick: "When it looked like I was lookin' here [he points in one direction], I was lookin' over there

[he points in a slightly different direction]. When it looked like I was lookin' over here [he points in a third direction], I was really lookin' at the judge. That's how I am."

However, Ricky does admit there were moments when his awareness of the trial proceedings slipped backward into his own thoughts. His voice has an engaging note of wistfulness when he says, "Sometimes I was—in a daze tryin' to figure out things. Sometimes I wasn't even there."

Perhaps because he was "confident in Mr. Kellam *all* the time," perhaps because he professes to have no prejudice against whites, Ricky states emphatically that he was not bothered by the total exclusion of blacks from the jury. (His father agrees—he "didn't worry about it"—but he also thinks, erroneously, that the fact of an all-white jury in a trial such as Ricky's could be used as the basis for an appeal.*)

As the trial progressed into the second week, Ricky's hopes continued to rise. He felt secure with "Mr. Singer pullin' the questions and Mr. Kellam askin' them." When, infrequently, one of them whispered to their client, it was to inquire of him: " 'What do you think? . . . How do you feel? . . . Do you see anything that you think can be of any help—anything new?' [But] everything I could come up with they had already wrote down."

Just once did Ricky feel that Kellam had not pushed far enough with a line of questioning: "When Jimmy was talkin' about the gun . . . I can't remember the question that I wanted him to ask, but anyway, Jimmy was talkin' and he [Kellam] stopped Jimmy from talkin' and I wanted Jimmy to go on talkin'. That's about the only time." (The gun Ricky is referring to here is the one Jimmy had when he was eleven years old, not the .38 he claimed to have seen Ricky carrying at the scene of the crime. Obviously Ricky wanted to hear—and wanted the jury to hear—more about Jimmy's "unsavory past.")

Ricky did not consider either Jimmy or Jennifer to be a

---

*Since legal requirements were met by the inclusion of a number of blacks in the panel from which the jury was chosen, the actual makeup of the jury would not be considered a prejudicial factor.

particularly damaging witness. He was sure the jury recognized that their stories did not jibe. It was when Clarissa took the stand that Ricky "got more worried. . . . She was tight all the way through, really, and that's when I was worried. . . . I don't know. It sounded believable. It sounded very believable. . . . Then when I heard the tape, I realized that she messed up." And at that point, Ricky thinks, everyone should have doubted her credibility as a witness to the crime.

When he speaks of his own testimony, the hostility he showed to Mendelow creeps back into his voice. "I said *around* four o'clock. And he tried to put me at four-ten on the dot. And I said *around* four, four-ten." He was so tense at this point that he did not hear the cry of "Right on, Ricky" from the spectator section of the courtroom and has no idea who was responsible for it. 'But today his judgment of Mendelow is relatively mild. "He's a creep," Ricky says, and laughs, but then he softens his verdict, or at least elaborates upon it. "He was doin' his job, I guess, but at the end he was goin' off a little bit . . . [when Mendelow warned the jury not to be swayed by sympathy for the defendant arising from his mother's death]. That's when Mr. Kellam said, 'I object.' It was during the summation. . . . That's when he was a creep."

Of Judge Agresta, Ricky says, "He did a fantastic job. He did a fantastic job of keeping the boringness away from the court. But the only thing I didn't like about him was when he made me laugh and I didn't wanna laugh." I assure Ricky that I never saw him laugh, not once.

When the jury began its deliberations, Ricky, with his attorneys' full encouragement, remained very hopeful. But the longer the jury was out, the more worried he became. The hours ticked by; he stalked his cell next to the courtroom. At some point he was brought downstairs for a meal. And then, in the middle of the evening—about eight or nine, he thinks—he suffered a rending shock and his hopes all but collapsed.

From the very beginning of his trial, every morning and night Ricky had been riding to and from the courthouse with a Puerto Rican youth of about eighteen or nineteen named—

something like—Pocheko. He was of course confined to Rikers Island, but Ricky did not know him from there. He was a police-van and courthouse-cell acquaintance and, like Ricky, he was on trial for murder—"something about a policeman," Ricky says disingenuously. Pocheko's trial went to the jury the same day as Ricky's, but his jury reached a verdict at least two hours earlier.

Ricky was waiting in the cell when Pocheko returned. He had been found guilty and faced a sentence of from twenty-five years to life. Ricky's voice is barely audible as he tells how Pocheko beat on the bars of the cell until his hands were cut and bloodied. Ricky watched in rising fear until he, too, in his own way could no longer contain himself. He broke into uncontrollable weeping. He just could not stop, not even when, a few moments later, guards took him from the cell and brought him back into the courtroom.

The jury had returned not to deliver a verdict, but to hear once again a portion of the testimony Clarissa had given on tape. Ricky sat at the defense table, head down, a handkerchief squeezed up against his eyes, his body quivering. It took about five minutes for the court reporter to read the taped passage that the jury had requested. Ricky was still crying when he was led back to the cell. Pocheko was gone.

In the courtroom at that time, in addition to the judge and the attorneys, the guards and the clerks and the jury, were Ricky's father, his sister Penny, his brother Warren, two aunts, and an uncle—perhaps other relatives as well; Ricky is not sure. Some if not all of them must have noticed he was crying. Certainly the two lawyers knew, but, Ricky murmurs, "They didn't know *why.* " And curiously, no one ever asked why until I did, and that was weeks later, when the trial had long been over.

The Journal of a Juror

Thursday, October 23, 1975

THE FINAL DAY

LAST NIGHT the Cincinnati Reds beat the Boston Red Sox in the seventh game of the World Series. So this morning we had something to talk about in the jury room besides the trial. It was a great game and a great series, Juror 2 and I agreed, at length. But talk of baseball could not overcome the tension that filled the room. Several people wondered aloud how long the day would be. Two women mentioned that they had brought along nightgowns, and they laughed. There was much speculation as to whether we would be charged before or after lunch. If the former, lunch would be paid for and, we thought, we would be taken to a restaurant *en masse*. All talk ended when we lined up in the corridor and filed into the courtroom. It was almost 10 A.M.

Kellam delivered his summation first. He was absolutely masterful. At least as much an actor or, more precisely, a thundering evangelist as an attorney, he gave a performance that lasted over an hour and kept me riveted for its entire length. His voice would drop to just above a whisper and then soar to what was almost a bellow. He gestured lavishly, pointing an accusing finger toward heaven itself and pounding his fist on the rail of the jury box as if he wanted to splinter it.

Throughout he focused on the weakness of the state's case;

122

rarely did he proclaim Ricky's innocence. Every inconsistency, contradiction, and improbability in the testimony of the three kids was exposed to his ridicule and contempt. At one point he shouted that if he thought Ricky had invited Jennifer to join him in the robbery and then later had stopped in his flight to show the kids his gun, then Kellam would have pleaded insanity as a defense. All the stunning conflicts in testimony about time and place and which of the three were present, including some that I had not thought of before, were reviewed, as was the police's failure to follow up on their many leads. What about "Brain" and "Savage"? What about the abandoned car? What about Mr. Simpkins in the hospital with a wound in his leg? He emphasized the pressure on the police to solve this crime, to get someone accused. He suggested that the kids may have borne ill will toward Ricky, reminding us of the broken-chair incident and the fact that Jimmy's mother had had the defendant's brother arrested. He came up with a striking new theory: that the kids had arrived at the scene of the crime sometime after the murder had been committed. This would explain why Jimmy had thought he heard broken glass (which he later decided was gunshots)—the police had to break the right front window of the van to get inside. It would explain why Clarissa said (on the tape and I had not caught it) that she was looking for a policeman to report her mother's accident and there were a lot of police around but she couldn't find one. It would explain why in their earliest statements to the police all the kids had insisted that they got to Murdock Avenue at five-thirty.

Kellam concluded with a poem entitled "Dream of Freedom," which he attributed to Langston Hughes. There were tears in his eyes as he spoke the last words. The judge recessed the court immediately after and as we filed out I noticed that Juror 9 was crying. With the gift of hindsight I would say now that Kellam's was an astonishingly effective performance for anyone already nurturing the seeds of doubt, but too emotional to persuade someone who was then strongly leaning toward a guilty verdict.

The recess was brief and again filled with speculation about meals. This ended with the arrival of the guard, Jack, to get our sandwich and beverage orders for lunch. We would hear the judge's charge before we ate and therefore the state would pay —but we were eating in, the meal to be catered by the Homestead [a gourmet food shop in Kew Gardens].

We were back in court around eleven-thirty, to hear Mendelow's summation. He showed far more passion than he ever had before, and indeed, given the crippled condition of his case, he thrust as much force and reason into his arguments as anyone reasonably could. His most telling points, for me, centered on Ricky's testimony: Where were the boys he had shot baskets with, where was this supposed girlfriend, how could Ricky not know the Murdock Avenue stores when for ten years he had lived only three blocks away. (Wasn't it about six blocks?) Mendelow said he could not produce a movie film of the crime being committed, but he had offered us the next best thing: *three* eyewitnesses. And their testimony, he vehemently repeated over and over and over, was overwhelming. Since he could not totally ignore the kids' inconsistencies, he whipped out the law-school experiment that proved how different people can see and remember the same sequence of events in entirely different ways. (Juror 6 brought this up at lunch yesterday.) He cried out that it would be "an insult to the intelligence of a sophisticated group" like us to suggest that the three kids would frame Ricky just for the money. Breaking down the sum into three hundred dollars per person (a questionable ploy; isn't it likely that if the reward were ever paid to the kids, the entire sum would actually go to Mrs. Custis?), he said these kids would have to be the lowest of the low to do something so vile. Did we really think that of them?

He began his summation by saying we all like poetry and Kellam's poem about dreams was very nice, but he reminded us that there was one person who would never dream again— Edward Fendt, the victim of this brutal murder. To Fendt he returned just before he concluded, emphasizing once again the utter horror of the crime. His last words reminded us of the promises we had made during the *voir dire:* not to be biased in the defendant's favor because of his age (to that he added the fact of Ricky's mother's death, which prompted a loud but futile objection from Kellam), not to demand more than proof beyond a reasonable doubt, not to be swayed by unsavory incidents in the past of his witnesses, and to use our common sense. If we remembered all those promises, he was sure we would find the defendant guilty as charged.

Both attorneys had prefaced their summations with expressions of gratitude for our attentiveness, but I noticed Juror 8 nodding off again—for just a few seconds—while Mendelow spoke.

His summation took about an hour and the judge's charge to the jury, which followed immediately, was almost as long. Agresta began by explaining that our purpose was to determine the facts of the case—to decide, by weighing and comparing the credibility of the various witnesses, whether the defendant had broken a law. It was not our function to question or interpret the law. Laws are made by our legislators and it is our job only to help enforce them. He continued with a thorough review of all the evidence that had been presented, witness by witness. He was remarkably fair and complete. He then went into a long and rather complicated explanation of the two counts of murder in the second degree: The first count, felony murder, referred to homicide committed during the course of an attempted robbery; the second, common law murder, was homicide with intent to kill. We could find the defendant guilty of either or both or neither. He said far more than I include here and I am giving short shrift to an outstanding, wholly admirable man (whatever else we may disagree about, we the jurors are unanimous in our praise for Agresta), but in view of the outcome of the jury's deliberations it seems superfluous to try to recall all his remarks. However enlightening they may have been as regards the law and however useful in recalling the substance of the trial testimony, in our deliberations there was scarcely any reference to Agresta's charge to the jury. Our verdict was determined by what we thought we heard from the witness box, not from the bench.

Our lunch was waiting for us when we returned to the jury room. It was immediately clear that we were all reluctant to begin deliberations and, in the easiest decision of the day, we chose not to until we had finished eating. Sandwiches were distributed about one-thirty. We ate in relative silence; then, rather elaborately and fastidiously, we gathered up the debris and cleared the table. At last, shortly before two o'clock, discussions began.

We asked first to see all the evidence that had been so frustratingly denied to us throughout the trial. It was brought into the jury room without delay, but strangely, it now seemed to me anticlimactic, a matter of curiosity rather than of pertinent interest. I thought to myself: So that's where the grocery store is. And the van *was* parked at almost the opposite corner from where Jennifer at first said the kids were standing when Ricky ran past them. And the picture of the suspect that Chris Borgen had shown on the Channel 2 News certainly looked nothing like the defendant. And, though the snapshots were quite blurred, that most assuredly was Ricky leaving the funeral home. And Edward Fendt, lying on the floor of his van in the blood that streamed from his temple, looked very dead indeed.

We read the police reports and the kids' statements. In black and white, the inconsistencies seemed no more or less glaring than when spoken on the witness stand. The many exhibits were passed around, conscientiously examined, commented upon, but it was all a holding action: much movement and exclamation and theorizing that served only to delay what we all sensed was inevitable conflict.

From just about the first significant words spoken, however, I knew, with a great rush of relief, that I would not be the lone holdout and that we would never declare Ricky guilty. Hung jury, perhaps. Guilty, no.

We did not start with a vote, but if we had I'm reasonably certain the outcome would have been as follows:

Juror   1—Not guilty
Juror   2—Undecided

Juror 3—Not guilty
Juror 4—Undecided
Juror 5—Guilty
Juror 6—Guilty
Juror 7—Undecided
Juror 8—Not guilty
Juror 9—Not guilty
Juror 10—Not guilty
Juror 11 (me)—Not guilty
Juror 12—Undecided

Those first significant words prompted not only relief but surprise, and the surprise stemmed not only from their content but from their source. They were spoken by, of all people, Juror 8—the former first alternate, the occasional snoozer, and the imitator, yesterday, of the young punk's walk. What he said—tersely, flatly, and with that somewhat choked quality fat men's voices sometimes have—was: "The state ain't got no case." Then there was silence in the room.

It was broken by Juror 1, our forewoman, and she proved the biggest surprise of all. She, who over eight days had smiled a lot and said very little, took command immediately and she was nothing short of remarkable. As we began deliberating, with the exhibits gathered up and put aside, she exchanged seats with Juror 5 and moved to the end of the table opposite me. From then on, where she sat became the head of the table.

She opened the discussion by asking Juror 8 if he wanted to elaborate on his statement. When he was unwilling or unable to do so, she turned to the rest of us: Would anyone volunteer his or her reconstruction of the case? Getting no immediate response, she proceeded to do it herself, and she stated my views almost exactly: she discounted all the police testimony as failing to implicate Ricky in any way; she reviewed the descriptions given by the adult eyewitnesses, particularly Clare Anderson, and reminded us that they did not resemble Ricky at all; therefore, she said, the state's case had to rest solely on the testimony of the three kids—and she for one could not believe it. She suggested that they were motivated by the promise of a reward—or perhaps for some other reason—but no matter what, to her their stories were transparent, and she went on to enumerate an inescapable series of flaws. She went further than I had in my mind by speculating that after the kids had spoken to the police, they realized they had embarked on a very dangerous course and now they were afraid. Perhaps they even regretted what they had done. Fear or regret or both would explain why they were reluctant witnesses. In any case, their testimony was so incredible that she would have to find Ricky not guilty.

She suggested then that we go around the table and each of us talk in turn. Juror 4, sitting to Juror 1's right, said he was undecided, Juror 8 in a minimum of words agreed with Juror 1, Juror 12 said he was bothered by things Ricky had said on the stand. There was silence again, and though I was not next around the table, I finally spoke up. I said I agreed with Juror 1 entirely, though I hadn't thought about the reasons the three kids were reluctant witnesses. I admitted right off that I was not at all certain that Ricky was innocent, but I was certain I couldn't convict him on the evidence offered. I listed the inconsistencies that bothered me the most in the kids' testimony (where they were when they observed the crime, what time it was, how many of them were there). I suggested that at some point they had decided Jimmy was too unreliable a witness and thus had to be separated from the two girls, though Clarissa's first police interview, one of the documents offered in evidence, revealed that she originally had Jimmy standing with her and Jennifer when they saw Ricky running from the truck.

Juror 3 spoke up and said that "deep in her gut" she suspected Ricky was "guilty as hell," but she was also sure that the kids were lying and therefore she had to vote not guilty. Juror 7 agreed and, soon, so did Juror 12. At this point there was a kind of informal voice vote: eight not guilty, two undecided (Jurors 4 and 2), and two guilty (Jurors 5 and 6). We had been deliberating for about an hour and a half.

Juror 2 found it difficult to believe that in "their ethnic

group" these kids would turn on one of their own and concoct such a story simply for the reward. He told us a rambling anecdote about a black man who had once worked with him and who had stood by another black in circumstances where no white man would have supported another white. I answered that it would be a miracle for us to *know* what may have motivated the kids—the range of human experience was just too broad and the possible explanations were endless. I mentioned a theory that had come to me a day or two before: What if Jennifer's boyfriend, whose name was mentioned during the trial, had been involved in the crime? What if the description of the suspect given on the Channel 2 News and the sketch shown had resembled this man? What if he had then taken off for Texas and the kids, to keep the police off his trail, had decided to implicate Ricky? (They had come forward no more than five days after that CBS News program.) There, certainly, was a motive for the kids. But no sooner had I offered this theory —and I could see some jurors nodding their heads in interest and others all set to attack it—than I disavowed it. It was pure conjecture, I said, unsupported by a crumb of evidence, but it was an example of the myriad of possible truths in this case.

The "not guilty" faction was strongly on the offensive at this point. Encouraged by the fact that we had already swayed two of the "undecideds," we hammered at two key arguments: Ricky's dissimilarity to the sketch of the suspect drawn from Clare Anderson's description and the unmistakable discrepancies between Clarissa's original police interview, her later interview (taped) with an assistant D.A., and her aborted testimony on the stand. I'm sure Jurors 4 and 2 were already leaning heavily toward the majority when they asked if we could hear Clarissa's tape again. This was quickly arranged. Our door was unlocked, from the outside, and we were brought back into the courtroom to have the tape replayed for us. The two "undecideds" had probably reached their verdict by the time we returned to the jury room. In any case, when we finally took our first paper ballot—it was now about 6 P.M.—the vote was ten to two. We had been deliberating for about four hours.

I have put off consideration of the arguments of the two holdouts, Jurors 5 and 6, because I know it will be a Herculean task to treat their views sympathetically, or at least dispassionately. It will be almost as difficult to communicate the mounting impatience and, ultimately, the rage that these men gave rise to. But it will be most difficult of all to dig into and expose the roots of the opposition with which they tried to "hang" us. Juror 5, probably the oldest person in the room, was convinced to the end that Ricky was guilty, but in objective terms he never really explained why. He kept alluding to "bad vibes" and to the "feeling in his gut"—he rarely went beyond the viscera to the brain. Thus, for as long as he was a holdout, he was mostly content to allow Juror 6 to do battle for them both. His occasional contributions were usually incorrect, irrelevant, or incredible. He forgot testimony, seemed incapable of understanding some of the arguments we offered, was mired in that "gut" certainty that Ricky was "guilty as hell" (how many times was that phrase used tonight—ten, fifteen, fifty?). His most astonishing statement: In response to someone's comment about how Kellam had badgered the three kids, I asked why Mendelow had pressed Ricky about his aunt's Brooklyn address. What did it prove that he didn't remember it? Answered Juror 5, "He said he went to Brooklyn on the day of the crime." Here was one person with freedom to dream.

Juror 6. Came to the U.S. from Czechoslovakia twenty-five years ago, a CPA with one of New York's largest accounting firms, a command of English—though he, like Juror 4, speaks with an accent—probably greater than that of anyone else in the jury room. Loquacious. Stentorian. Ready with an anecdote on any subject. A self-proclaimed expert on gourmet cooking, the stock market, and—so unfortunately for the rest of us—guns and human nature. He announced early on that he had made a significant discovery: the bullet wounds evident in the photographs of the deceased proved that he was hit by very rapid shots. Therefore, though as many as twelve shots may have been fired, by murderer and victim combined, it was quite possible that the kids thought they heard only two. No one had even brought up this discrepancy, but he aired his refutation of it regularly, each time as if it were a major finding.

On human nature, or more precisely black human nature, he knew more than the rest of us because he sees blacks socially. His first memorable statement once deliberations began: "I am sorry there are no blacks on this jury." Because blacks know how other blacks think. Said Juror 1, then, and repeatedly over the next nine hours, "Phillip, we shouldn't, we mustn't, talk about color." Juror 6 smiled condescendingly. At one point I mentioned one of Jennifer's most astonishing statements: that she and Clarissa and Jimmy had *never* discussed among themselves seeing Ricky commit the crime, not even after their mother gathered them into her car and drove them to the precinct house to talk to the police. "What wheels turning in her head could make her think that we would believe something like that?" I asked, rhetorically. Juror 6 announced, "Black wheels."

He had quickly conceded that the kids' testimony was full of contradictions. But that didn't trouble him. He had a theory: the four of them were in it together. They had all attempted to rob—and succeeded in murdering—the potato chip man. But a month later something happened—perhaps the offer of a reward, perhaps something else—to cause Jennifer, Clarissa, and Jimmy to decide to make Ricky their scapegoat. In effect, then, all the blacks were guilty, but since only one was on trial, he could convict only one.

There were three "facts" he considered irrefutable: they all said they saw Ricky leaning half in, half out of the truck, they all heard the shots, they all saw the gun. With glee he reminded us that they described the gun differently: Jimmy said it was a .38, Jennifer said it was "little and brownish," Clarissa said it was "medium and brown." But these inconsistencies *proved* they were telling the truth because the kids weren't *experts* and they couldn't tell one gun from another.

For every other inconsistency, contradiction, or improbability he attempted to offer an answer. Failure of memory over so long a period, failure of perception in the excitement of the

moment, or—when he was truly desperate—"That's not important"; "That doesn't bother me. I can live with it." What he
could not live with would be his conscience if he allowed this
killer to go free.

What about the eyewitness descriptions given by the adults
on the day of the crime? Particularly Clare Anderson's description and the sketch that was drawn from it. Juror 6: "They all
said the murderer was black, didn't they?" But in hardly any
other way did their descriptions correspond to Ricky, and Clare
Anderson, who claimed to have actually faced the man for a
second or two, could not identify Ricky in the line-up. Juror 6:
"She was frozen with fear and shock and in such a state perceptions are meaningless." It seemed he could not be moved.

But he could be caught. At one point, after a long, aimless
pause in the deliberations, Juror 6 said with a sly smile, "You all
keep asking me to explain to you why I think Ricky is guilty.
Well, now I ask you: How can you prove to me that he is
innocent?" Without a breath of hesitation—almost as if she had
been waiting for this question—Juror 1 met the challenge:
"Phillip, we don't have to prove he is innocent. He is *presumed*
innocent. That's our system here. The prosecution has to prove
him guilty." Juror 6's smile faded but did not disappear. Was he
embarrassed by his unthinking lapse? He conceded nothing.
The smile became a look of condescension, as if to say, "And
that, my dear, is what is wrong with your system."

It was close to 7 P.M. when Juror 1 reminded us of the
theory Kellam had introduced in his summation: that the kids
arrived at the crime scene *after* the murder was committed.
This would explain why Jimmy said he heard glass breaking,
why Clarissa said there were a lot of cops around but she
couldn't find one to whom to report her mother's accident, why
all three *originally* told the police they saw Ricky commit the
crime about five-thirty. On the second point, said Juror 5, "I
never heard her say that"; said Juror 6, "That isn't exactly what
she said." Juror 1: "Yes, it is. We heard it again on the tape this
afternoon—'There were a lot of cops around but I couldn't find
one.' Would you like to have the tape played for us again?" We

agreed to ask for the transcript (actually, the court reporter's record) of the tape.

Juror 1: "What about their insistence in their early testimony that it all happened at five-thirty?" Juror 6: "They didn't have watches." Juror 1: "But Detective McKinley testified that when he interviewed Clarissa she at first insisted that she saw Ricky at *five-thirty*, even after he reminded her that the murder was committed at five." (Now how did she remember that? She's brilliant.) Juror 6: "I don't remember that." Juror 5: "I don't either."

We agreed to ask to have that bit of testimony read back to us also. We summoned Jack, who took our request and then told us we would soon be going out to dinner. "You're eating Italian tonight." Italian in that neighborhood probably meant Luigi's, where I hadn't been in years.

The prospect of soon leaving this smoky, supercharged room served to reduce the tension. Juror 5 admitted that he would have to be influenced by Clarissa's reference to "a lot of cops around" if that proved to be what she said on the tape.

After more than six hours in the jury room, we were finally released and taken to dinner. We were accompanied by four guards, including one woman, in case any of the female jurors had to use the bathroom in the restaurant. We were admonished not to speak or wave to anyone we might know on the street. We marched out of the courthouse two abreast.

It was an uncommonly warm evening for late October, but it felt wonderful to breathe the fresh, however polluted, air of Kew Gardens. Luigi's is about two blocks west. As we walked there I overheard not one word about the trial and that remained true after we were seated at our table at the rear of the restaurant. (The guards had their own table, adjacent to ours.) We had been instructed to order no more than five dollars' worth of food (the wide-ranging effects of the fiscal crunch), which meant that we had to ignore the $6.95 *table d'hôte* half of the menu.

Dinner conversation was relaxed; jovial, in fact. The two holdouts were at opposite ends of the table, Juror 6 at my end, indeed directly opposite me. But there was no mention of the disagreement that had raged between us and would again. Instead four of us talked, surprisingly, of politics (Juror 6 abhors Hubert Humphrey; Juror 4 remarked that though he votes Republican 75 percent of the time, he just can't tolerate Ford), of book publishing (Juror 12, to my left, could not believe how low is the average first printing of a book), of travel (Juror 12 has been to Scandinavia, Juror 4 to Italy). The food was mediocre, the coffee no better, but we lingered over it, reluctant to return to battle. It was close to 9 P.M. when the guards led us back to the courthouse, stopping traffic for us twice along the way. (Quite a feat on Queens Boulevard.) As I mounted the steps (last in line going to the restaurant, I was first coming back), I looked up to the second floor of the darkened building. In a window directly above I could discern the figures of Kellam, Singer, and Ricky's father, peering down at us. If they wondered what we were talking about as we re-entered the courthouse, would they have been disappointed or amused to know that Juror 9 and I were discovering that her mother and my in-laws live only a few miles apart in Florida?

The jury room was no more inviting on our return than it had been when we left, but we were not in it very long before we were recalled to the courtroom, to rehear the testimony we had requested. As we crossed to the jury box and I passed Ricky sitting at the defense table, I noticed that, for the first time, he appeared to be crying. At least he was holding a white handkerchief to his eyes and there it remained for as long as the jury sat in the courtroom.

The court reporter read Clarissa's taped testimony as he had recorded it. Loudly, distinctly, his voice a monotone, he recited: "There were lots of cops around but I couldn't find one." The words were indeed Clarissa's, and though they were now spoken without expression or stress, they seemed far more dramatic and telling than when we had heard them before, in her own small, breathy, barely audible tape-recorded voice. I looked at Juror 5 but could see only his profile, which stared ahead impassively.

After reading the taped testimony in its entirety, the court reporter found that isolated passage from Kellam's cross-examination of Detective McKinley. There could be no doubt now. McKinley had flatly admitted that when Clarissa was first questioned she stuck to five-thirty as the time she saw Ricky running away, even after she was told that the potato chip man had been murdered much closer to five o'clock. Kellam was right. He had to be right. All three kids had initially given five-thirty as the crucial time simply because that was the time of Mrs. Custis's car accident and the accident was the anchor of reality to which their story was tied. We would never know who, or what, later caused them to move the time of their arrival on Murdock Avenue to five o'clock. But originally all three had clung to that one shred of truth—five-thirty in the afternoon.

Back in the jury room, I knew it was merely a matter of time before Juror 5 abandoned his ally. The immediate response was from Juror 6: Hearing the testimony again had not swayed him at all. He knew even before this last excursion to the courtroom *exactly* what had been said, and it made no difference to him. Was it at this point or earlier that, dropping his voice to just above a whisper, he confessed that the "vibes" from Ricky were what had persuaded him that the boy was a killer? With the kids' stories crumbling around him, he moved to a clearer spot: the testimony, and, more important, the demeanor of Ricky on the stand. The kid was arrogant, he was hostile, he was evasive. Couldn't we all tell he was guilty?

Juror 5 could tell. Of course Ricky was guilty. He had that feeling in his gut. But he had to admit now there *was* a doubt. The state's case was weak. Yes, Ricky was guilty, guilty as hell —but he was changing his vote. Sadly but with a kind of flourish. He wanted the respect that age commands. He got a few smiles at least. For now it was eleven to one. We had been deliberating for over eight hours.

Instead of bringing relief, the capitulation of Juror 5 recharged the atmosphere. The pressure on Juror 6 should have been insupportable. But without any evident rancor toward the sudden renegade, he made it immediately clear that *he* was not planning to change *his* vote, now or in the future. Anger burst around him. He was being totally unreasonable. How could he still insist on "guilty" when the state's case had been exposed to him, over and over again, as a fraud? What more could any of us say? He repeated, with that exasperated but not yet spent patience that teachers show to mischievous children, "I don't care about the kids' stories. Sure, they may be lying. But not about the important thing. Ricky is on trial, not the kids."

There seemed to be no more avenues of attack open to us. We had tried to wear him down by confronting him with all the flaws in the kids' testimony, but he had made it inescapably clear that this strategy was futile. I sat silently for a moment, trying to come up with a new argument, yet certain that it would prove as useless as all the others.

I thought to myself: He believes all four were conspirators in the crime. Can we build on that? Of course! Trying to keep my voice down and free of hostility, I asked Juror 6 how he could be sure, if they were all in it together, that it was Ricky rather than one of the other three who had pulled the trigger. Someone else answered, "It couldn't have been one of the girls." Had I believed the shared-guilt theory, I would not have conceded even that, but for the moment it didn't matter. "Just Jimmy, then. How do you know Jimmy didn't do it?" "Because," replied Juror 6, "the description of the killer given by the four adults sounded much more like Ricky." "But you've already said we should discount their statements. They were in shock or too frightened to be reliable witnesses. You can't have it both ways—dismissing what they said when it favors Ricky and accepting it when it doesn't!" Silence again and then a barely audible remark from Juror 6: "Let me sleep on it."

For me this was the first hopeful note of the evening, but to my surprise, I was virtually alone in my reaction. The others seemed more irate at the implied suggestion that we be sequestered overnight than they were by the possibility of our never reaching a verdict. Indeed, the sense of outrage now was almost palpable. "That's so unfair. That's so selfish!" shouted Juror 3, sitting to my right—she who had, for the past week, talked about little except her home and family. She whispered to me that the time had come for us to report to the judge that we were at an impasse. "Let it be a hung jury and let's go home," she said. I answered that it was very likely that the judge would insist that we continue to deliberate. "But how can he do that?" she whined. Around us indignation was boiling. The surrender of Juror 5 had proved to be like the dropping of a single shoe. Everyone had waited for the second to fall and now frustration was more intense than it had ever been, for it appeared that the shoe would not fall tonight.

Somehow, by offering the faint suggestion that he might *eventually* change his mind, Juror 6 seemed more stubborn, quixotic, and self-indulgent than he had when he was proclaiming that he would never vote for acquittal. Shouts of abuse and personal hostility were coming from jurors who for hours had said almost nothing. At some point, much earlier, Juror 7 had observed that Juror 6 and I were the most diametrically opposed. I questioned that at the time (and still do) because it seemed to me that the forewoman was at least as firm in her verdict of not guilty as I was. Now, however, there was no doubt that both Juror 6 and I were together in misjudging the mood of the others. His offer to "sleep on it," intended no doubt to reduce the pressure on him and welcomed by me as cause for optimism, had only served to isolate him further from the group. The barrage of arguments and supplications—the same arguments and the same supplications that had been voiced for hours—was now impelled by a renewed rush of anger.

Which only served to stiffen his resistance. Did he immediately regret his vague concession? Perhaps. For when the forewoman, with her own blend of exasperation and studied calm, asked if there was any real possibility that he would ever change his mind, he replied, almost smugly, that it was very remote. And then he added, in a thundering voice, "Only I have to live with my conscience!" The massive egotism here—as if everyone else's conscience were some muddy mess and his were granite—produced another uproar. It was interrupted by a knock on the door and the arrival of the judge's assistant.

He immediately made it clear that Agresta would not accept a "no verdict" decision tonight. If we couldn't come to
unanimous agreement soon, we would have to be put up at a
hotel to resume deliberations in the morning. What had been
the effect, he wanted to know, of the reading of the testimony
after dinner? Juror 1 explained that it had changed one vote
and we now stood eleven to one. "Well, keep trying," he said
as he walked to the door. We had been deliberating for almost
nine hours.

Alone again, our mood seemed to change from anger to
resignation and disgust. To many, I'm sure, every road seemed
blocked and every weapon spent. But the forewoman was determined to try again, and I tried to help her. Between us we
reviewed once more all the reasons for our own doubts: the
adult descriptions that in no significant way resembled Ricky,
Clarissa's remark about the police, the conflicts in time and
place, the wild improbabilities, the general sense of untruth
that had settled crushingly on the testimony of the three kids.
I added a new note, in desperation and regret, for I wanted to
persuade Juror 6 by rational arguments and not by group pressure: We were eleven fairly intelligent, fairly perceptive people. Didn't the fact that we all agreed on not guilty—that we
all thought there were grounds for a reasonable doubt—didn't
that mean anything to him? I could not hear his reply, for other
voices were drowning out mine even before I finished my question. And most powerful among those voices was that of Juror
5. "There is a reasonable doubt!" he cried. The next-to-last
holdout had joined the pack and at that moment the pack was
immeasurably strengthened.

Was what followed the most sustained barrage of the evening? Had some sort of climax been reached? Yes, the voices
were rising again, but were they actually louder and sharper
than ever before? Perhaps Juror 6 only thought they were. How
much pressure can one man take? Suddenly, he broke.

"All right," he said, almost softly. "I've come to respect all
of you too much. I can't do this to you and I won't continue any
longer. I change my vote."

Juror 1 started to cry. I felt limp and choked. "Christ almighty, we did it. We did it," I said to myself. But within seconds Juror 6 had leaped to his feet, his eyes blazing, and like a titan of vengeance, tottering and about to collapse, he screamed at us all: *"And how many of you believe with me that we are turning an animal loose on the streets again?"* It seems almost comical now to remember that two or three hands shot up immediately—such a puny gesture in response to such Jehovic wrath. Said Juror 2, "If you add the word 'possibly' . . ." But Juror 6 was not adding anything. He was stumbling away from the table and toward the bathroom, his eyes flooded with tears.

Juror 1 rang the bell and Jack opened the door at once. He smiled when he heard that we had reached a verdict. As he went to report this to the court, we got to our feet. We were exhausted, in every way. Conversation was desultory. In the back of my mind there was a sense of triumph but not of elation, and I felt no comfort at all. Jack returned and had us line up in the hall. We left the jury room at ten forty-five. We had been in there for almost ten hours.

Cleaning men were sweeping the corridors as we waited to file into the courtroom for the last time. While in the past when we crossed to the jury box, I tended to avoid looking at Ricky, his lawyers, and the assistant D.A., now I gazed at them all, and saw nothing.

We stood at our places in the box and enacted the familiar last rite of all the stage, movie, and TV trials I've ever seen. Judge Agresta: "Ladies and gentlemen of the jury, have you reached a verdict?"

Juror 1: "We have, Your Honor."

Clerk of the court: "The defendant will rise and face the jury." (Ricky did, but the defense table was set at an angle to the jury box, and standing in front of his chair he may have faced Jurors 1 and 7, but he didn't face me.) "What is your verdict?"

Juror 1: "We find the defendant not guilty . . . on both counts."

As if he had just been shot, Ricky seemed to crumple and his body toppled over to his right. His arms went out to Kellam, for support and embrace. As he fell on his lawyer, he buried his face in Kellam's shoulder and he sobbed.

Said Judge Agresta, "Young man, every day of your life you should thank your attorney. That was one of the most brilliant defenses I've seen in my career."

Said Kellam, "Thank you, Judge." He smiled broadly, Ricky's head still on his shoulder.

The judge then turned to the questions he had earlier promised to answer when the trial was over. The original eighth juror had taken a sleeping pill the previous Wednesday night and had not awakened until late the next day. "I still haven't decided what to do about him." The various delays in the trial were caused by the difficulty in getting the three important state witnesses to appear: one [Jennifer] had to be brought from Texas, another [Jimmy] had to be picked up by the police, the third [Clarissa] had to be brought from the hospital. Once again we were thanked and wished a safe journey home, but this time the judge checked to make sure that all the women jurors had rides. On the way back to the jury room, I heard Juror 6, walking well ahead of me, say, "For the first time in twenty years I feel like a Judas." Who or what, I wondered, had he betrayed then?

In the jury room, as we picked up our belongings, Juror 7 said, "If we should ever get into trouble we should all remember that name. Kellam." Again there was something we all agreed about.

Down the hall to the elevator, down the elevator to the lobby, across the lobby to the main doors of the courthouse, and there Kellam was waiting. He shook our hands and thanked us all. Some of the jurors continued down the steps, but others hung back. There were two questions I had to ask Kellam: Had Ricky been in jail since last November? "Oh, sure; how could he raise that kind of money? Bail was set at fifty thousand bucks." Was Kellam a court-appointed lawyer? He nodded. Another juror asked, "Legal Aid?" No, he was in private practice. Then on the steps of the courthouse, a group of us gathered around Kellam and from all sides there were questions. And up the steps from the sidewalk came Singer.

For close to forty-five minutes the two attorneys answered questions and asked a few of their own.

"Why did Ricky have two lawyers?" Because Singer, the first court-appointed attorney (also in private practice), had become seriously ill in the spring and entered the hospital in July. Kellam was asked by the court to take over the defense. But Singer had become very attached to the case and when he recovered he asked if he could continue as Kellam's assistant.

"Why wasn't Louella Johnson called to the stand to support Ricky's story of what he had been doing on that afternoon?" Because she had told the defense she couldn't remember that day and it was dangerous to have her testify and offer her to the prosecution's attack.

"What important information weren't we given?" A couple of the kids had Family Court records. (Added Kellam, "They're real baaad, those kids.")

"Did the defense anticipate the verdict?" When we asked to hear the tape replayed, they figured we'd go for not guilty or be a hung jury. That tape turned out to be the most important piece of evidence they had, but they didn't even know of its existence until yesterday, the day we first heard it played. Even Mendelow didn't know about it before that morning, and the only reason he allowed it to be played was that Clarissa couldn't continue on the stand.

"Why didn't you let Mendelow ask Jennifer that question about why she waited so long to go to the police with her story?" Because her answer could have opened up a real can of worms. She could have made all sorts of statements in response to that that the defense was totally unprepared to handle.

"How much will you [Kellam] get paid?" It was completely up to the court and he was not sure. But the last time he was the court-appointed attorney in a murder case, which went on much longer than this one, the judge awarded him eight hundred dollars.

"Will the murder investigation be reopened now?" No, there are too many other unsolved crimes to worry about. Maybe someday the police will pick someone up on another charge and try to pin this one on him too. That's the only possibility.

"Were there any jurors you thought were against you?" Kellam smiled and pointed a finger at me. Everyone started to laugh. "I was worried about you." The laughter increased. "I didn't think I had you until sometime in my summation and then I saw something in your eye and I knew I gotcha!" Said Juror 9, "Were you wrong about him!"

I didn't hear the question and I don't know who asked it, but it must have been something like "Was Ricky really innocent?" And I heard Kellam's answer: "I was appointed late to this case because Steve got sick. And when I walked into that cell—he'd been in jail for about eight months—and I looked at Ricky and he looked at me and he said, 'Mr. Kellam, I didn't do it'—then I knew *in my gut* that he was innocent."

It was close to midnight when I got a cab and went home.

DREAM OF FREEDOM

There is a dream in the land with its
  back against the wall
By muddled names and strange, sometimes
  the dream is called.
There are those who claim this dream for
  theirs alone;
A sin for which we know they must atone.
Unless shared in common like sunlight and
  like air,
The dream will die for lack of substance
  anywhere.

This dream knows no frontier or tongue;
The dream no class or race.
The dream cannot be left secure in
  any one locked place.
The dream today embattled with its back
  against the wall,
To save the dream for one, it must be
  saved for all.

PART FIVE

The Final Witness

Q: The trial of Darrell Mathes ended many months ago and you have no doubt been discussing it freely since then. What is the question you are most often asked about the case?

A: Do I think the defendant really was innocent? Or the same question phrased differently: Don't I think the defendant really was guilty?

Q: How do you answer?

A: I say that during the trial and throughout the jury's deliberations, I was not at all convinced that Ricky was innocent —but I am now. There were three reasons for my original doubts. First the fact that Ricky's alibi was pathetically feeble, so feeble that it was virtually nonexistent. His inability to present a single witness to testify as to his whereabouts on the afternoon of the murder seemed to me, at that time, damagingly suspect. The second problem was Ricky himself. His demeanor in the courtroom and particularly on the witness stand was for many members of the jury just short of an admission of guilt. For me he did nothing to inspire belief in his credibility or convey in the slightest the minimal sense of responsibility one might expect from an adolescent. Finally, there stood the three supposed "eyewitnesses" who, in the very act of coming forward, cast a shadow on Ricky Mathes that nothing could entirely dissipate. However inconsistent their testimony, however unattractive they appeared to me as individuals, my mind balked at the idea that they would frame a kid for murder for no other apparent reason than the promise of a thousand-dollar

147

reward. In the light of the case the state presented, my doubts and questions were never strong enough for me to contemplate voting for a "guilty" verdict. But they were certainly sufficiently troubling for me to wonder, when the trial was over, whether, in terms of ultimate truth, justice had been done.

Q: And now?

A: I have known Ricky for nine months, have spent countless hours with him, and I am absolutely certain that he did not commit the crime. I do not pretend that my insight into the way he lives is wide or deep—my background and my values are too foreign to his to allow my ever knowing or understanding him fully—but some aspects of his life are clear to me and I daresay that I am as familiar as anyone with the personality he projects to the white world. I know his days are so barren and unchanging that, at any time, he would find it almost impossible to remember vividly or in detail what he did or whom he was with on a particular day a month before. I know that, under most circumstances, when he is in the company of white people he acts as if he feels threatened. He denies that he feels this way, but he cannot deny the appearance he gives—withdrawn, sullen, uncommunicative—the darting eyes, the restless fingers, the painful unease. All these characteristics, which to the jury suggested falsehood and guilt, are apparent when he sits down to dinner with my family or when he talks to me about his future. "That's how I am," Ricky says often, and that is indeed how he is. (His manner, however, and not surprisingly, is noticeably warmer and more relaxed when white people are with him in his own home.)

So the implications of Ricky's behavior and testimony in court, implications which, to varying degrees, all the members of the jury perceived, are now to my mind exposed as meaningless. They lead nowhere except back to their source, Ricky himself.

To support my certainty of Ricky's innocence I can also point to some facts that we as jurors were not aware of: he rejected outright any consideration of plea bargaining even though his lawyer made a case for it; he was regarded by neighbors of the Mathes family as a good kid who stayed out of trouble; his conduct during his incarceration was, by Rikers Island standards, almost exemplary. Furthermore, he has had no run-ins with the law since his acquittal, at this point almost a year ago.

But ultimately, my total confidence in the justness of our verdict rests on what Juror 5 would call "vibes." In coming to know Ricky I have come to recognize that he could no sooner plan and commit a one-man armed robbery than he could explain the theory of relativity. His total passivity (at least until provoked), his lack of ambition and drive, his weary acceptance of his lot whatever and wherever it may be, all combine to belie a capability for crime—except perhaps in reaction to what he feels is an offense against himself.

Q: And what of the three "eyewitnesses"—can you better explain their motive in offering false testimony?

A: I'm afraid that will always remain something of a mystery. However, I am now much less resistant to the theory that the three kids did it simply for the money. My limited research in the district attorney's files on the case revealed an occurrence that was never mentioned during the trial, and indeed was unknown to the defense. Lettie Lou Custis, mother or surrogate mother to the "eyewitnesses," volunteered to pay a "condolence call" on the Mathes family strictly to find out for the police exactly where and when Livvie's funeral was to be held (this to give the police an opportunity to take identification photographs of the boy Mrs. Custis's children had already identified as the murderer). The implications in this gesture of aid extend clearly and directly to the promise of the reward and suggest a single-minded determination to obtain it.

Perhaps bad feelings between members of Ricky's family and one or more of the "eyewitnesses" were a contributing factor too. But aside from the incidents mentioned in court (the warrant Jimmy's mother swore out for Joseph Mathes's arrest, and the broken chair), Ricky claims to know nothing that would support this possibility.

Q: You mention having done some research in the district attorney's office. Why?

A: For me, in retrospect, the most extraordinary aspect of

the trial was the weakness of the state's case. As Juror 8 said when we began our deliberations, "The state ain't got no case"; while this was not a unanimous view, it was certainly the opinion of at least six of us. And of the remaining six, five and perhaps all six were willing to consider a "guilty" verdict, not truly because of any evidence presented by the prosecutor but because the defendant himself, in his bearing and in his testimony, seemed to them to defy his own claim of innocence.

The first part of the prosecution's evidence was meager. Aside from establishing that the murderer was obviously black, the police testimony in no way implicated Ricky, at least not until Detective McKinley brought us to Jennifer, Clarissa, and Jimmy. Indeed, the early witnesses, with their hearsay descriptions of suspects that scarcely resembled the defendant, probably strengthened the *defense.* Therefore, the state's case rested on—or, more accurately, consisted wholly of—the testimony of the three teen-agers, kids who, from the outset, appeared to *every* member of the jury untrustworthy, unreliable, and unwholesome. But beyond that and more important, the words these witnesses spoke were so fraught with discrepancies that they relentlessly challenged belief. Why, then, I wanted to know, did the state bring this case to court? I thought that by examining the district attorney's files I might find out.

Q: Did you?

A: Not really. The file, at least six inches thick, bulges with police reports and photographs, only a few of which were introduced into evidence at the trial. It reveals that the police had a substantial number of leads during October and November of 1974, none of them particularly promising, some of them followed through to a dead end, more of them still active at the time the three kids came forward. But at that point all other lines of inquiry appear to have stopped: The police and the district attorney's office concentrated all their attention on these newly arrived "eyewitnesses." While Jennifer, Clarissa, and Jimmy were subjected to several interviews, over a period of a few days, there is nothing in the file to suggest that a strenuous effort was mounted to verify or corroborate or, indeed, to refute the kids' stories by further investigation. Two small moves were made in this direction. A twelve-year-old boy who, three days after the murder, had given the police a description of a suspect was asked to look at "several photos of male blacks [in] which a photo of the perpetrator . . . was included [and] did not pick out or identify the perpetrator as the person . . . he had seen in the vicinity of the crime scene on 10–14–74." The second attempt had the same result: Clare Anderson, at one time considered the most reliable of the eyewitnesses, was brought to the line-up and she also, as I already knew, failed to identify Ricky as the person she had seen fleeing from the potato chip truck. Curiously enough, to the D.A.'s office her failure to make the identification seems to have suggested not that the kids' testimony was perhaps suspect, but that Ms. Anderson was somehow wanting as a witness. Thus, some days after Ricky's arrest, the police visited her again, only to be informed that she had told them all she could and would no longer offer them any cooperation. Thereupon, for all practical purposes, the investigation was closed, and although, with Ricky's acquittal, the murder of Edward Fendt must officially be considered unsolved, it remains closed today.

I thought that in the district attorney's file I might find some evidence, inadmissible at the trial, that would confirm the kids' stories or in some other way allude to Ricky's guilt: a fact, an opinion, an observation from a source other than Jennifer, Clarissa, or Jimmy. I found nothing of the kind. The entire case the state had was the case it presented to the jury. Weren't its weaknesses—the contradictions, the inconsistencies, the reversals in the kids' statements—glaringly evident to these professional lawmen? Apparently not. Or maybe, as Kellam charged in his summation, the police and the district attorney's office were so eager, so desperate, to "solve" this murder case that they clutched at a straw, believing their victim so feeble that a straw would suffice.

Q: If the state's case was inadequate to begin with, do you feel it was strengthened or further weakened by the way in which it was presented in court?

A: I think that Mendelow did as well as could be expected, no better, no worse. He was handicapped by, of all things, a lack of familiarity with the case. Since I was completely uninformed as to the organization and procedures followed by a county district attorney's office, I was astonished to discover that Mendelow had been assigned to the Darrell Mathes trial long after the investigation had ended. He had not been present at any of the interrogations of the kids and, I have good reason to believe, had not even met them until shortly before they were called to the witness stand.

From the defense attorneys I learned the almost incredible fact that Mendelow did not know of the existence of the tape of Clarissa's interview until after her sudden illness prompted the judge to excuse her from testifying further. At that point, with no one able to predict when Clarissa would be well enough to resume, with Kellam insisting that he be allowed to continue his cross-examination, and with Agresta impatient to conclude the trial, someone from the district attorney's office produced the tape and offered it to the defense "in exchange for" having Clarissa recalled to the stand. The tape was played and it was then that Mendelow heard it for the first time. I do not know if he recognized immediately how damaging to his case the tape was. (When the defense attorneys first heard it, even they did not appreciate the full significance of Clarissa's remark: "There were lots of cops around but I couldn't find one.") But Kellam did catch enough discrepancies in her statements to accept the tape as a serviceable substitute for the live witness. Mendelow, however he may have judged the value of this previously unknown evidence, had no choice but to accept it. Thus, although the decision to play the tape for the jury was to prove fatal for him, it was a decision that circumstances demanded.

In the early days of the trial, I considered it a mistake for Mendelow to refer repeatedly to the "unsavory pasts" of his star witnesses and to their failure to come forward until a month after the crime was committed. Clearly he was trying to counter the jury's disapproval and distrust by anticipating it, but it seemed to me a transparent, ineffective tactic and one that emphasized rather than reduced the obstacles the district attorney faced. In retrospect, I don't think it made much difference. No matter what ploys he resorted to, Mendelow could no sooner have changed the jury's perception of the three kids than Kellam could have made us see Ricky as "the boy next door." When Mendelow had his witnesses on the stand, he treated them gently, warmly, deferentially. He never betrayed the fact that they were virtual strangers to him and he elicited from them enough information to build his case but not so much that they were likely to fall into self-created traps of inconsistency and contradiction. That was left for Kellam to lead them to do.

If Mendelow handled his own witnesses with care, he showed no concern at all for Ricky's sensibilities. The harshness of his attack in cross-examination of the defendant succeeded in exposing to the jury all Ricky's hostility and anger. It did not require much talent to uncover the void that was Ricky's alibi; where Mendelow demonstrated his capability was in how he played his strongest card, the personality of the defendant.

Mendelow, then, was good with witnesses, and he was equally good in his summation. Neither naturally eloquent nor flamboyant, he did manage to muster reserves of intense moral outrage as he pleaded with us to find Darrell Mathes guilty. He dressed the broken and jagged bones of his case in a costume of words that, at moments, managed to conceal just how paltry those bones were. No, his evidence was not "overwhelming," his witnesses—"eyewitnesses"—were not the "best kind of witness," and we the jury were not a "highly sophisticated" group. But he made his claims with spirit and apparent conviction, and, for the most part, it was not his fault that they were baseless.

Q: Since the state's case was feeble and in your opinion the prosecutor was something less than a legal giant, can we assume that the defense did not face a particularly stiff challenge in achieving an acquittal?

A: Paradoxically, no. In the beginning, when Singer was

first appointed defense counsel, the challenge was staggering. With no helpful information coming from either his client or the district attorney's office, Singer could scarcely see a reason for hope, let alone for acquittal. Only by doggedly searching and probing could he discern the outline of the state's case and surmise its weaknesses. It was at the Wade Hearing, five months after he was assigned to the case, that Singer first saw and heard the star witnesses; until that point he was actually a man fighting in the dark, not knowing who or where his opponent was.

By the time Kellam took over for Singer, a good deal of light had been shed: the Wade Hearing was over and 128 documents, almost entirely police investigation reports, had been turned over to the defense by the district attorney's office. In carefully combing these reports, particularly the summaries of the kids' statements and the transcript of a taped interview with Jennifer, the lawyers met a substantial part of the initial challenge. They learned enough to devise a courtroom strategy.

Once the trial began, carrying out that strategy held its own potential pitfalls. Kellam's job was to destroy the credibility of the star witnesses. In their pretrial statements and in their answers during cross-examination he found the means to do this, but because these witnesses were young, he had to guard against incurring the jury's sympathy for them by appearing to badger or harass or abuse them. Kellam walked this fine line well if not perfectly.

Finally, there remained the challenge posed by the nature of the defendant. Ricky earnestly protested his innocence, but everything else about him was a problem: his age, his color, his personality, his "alibi." Both his attorneys sensed the effect he would have on a jury and until the end of the trial it was their responsibility—a heavy one—to make sure that Ricky did not hang himself.

Q: Do you, then, think the defense made a tactical error in putting Ricky on the stand?

A: That's an interesting question, one that can never be satisfactorily answered. The fact is, of course, that a majority of the jury had strong doubts about Ricky's innocence even while they were voting to acquit, and as we know, it was largely Ricky himself who was responsible for this. Largely but not entirely, for Ricky could not change the color of his skin, or the severity of New York's crime problem, or the suspicion with which whites see blacks. And I am convinced that these factors alone would have influenced the judgment of some of the jurors and perhaps the deliberations of the jury as a whole. Thus, even if Ricky had not testified in his own defense—and the jury had known him only as the tall, skinny, poker-faced young black who sat sprawled at the defense table—he would, to an incalculable extent, have been the victim of fears and prejudices beyond his control.

Furthermore, if he had not been called to the stand, the effect of his failure to testify would inevitably have been highly damaging. Constantly during the *voir dire* we had been reminded that the defendant was not legally obligated to appear as a witness, but knowing the jurors, I can safely say that a number of them—those who were willing to make extreme allowances for the kids' lack of credibility—were silently demanding that Ricky take the stand. Had he not done so, for them he would have come close to making a confession of guilt. I can almost hear them in the jury room asking why he had not spoken up for himself. What did he have to hide? Why couldn't he dispute what the kids had said? And to those questions his supporters in the jury room would have had no answers at all. So while the testimony Ricky gave and the personality he exhibited were harmful to his cause, his silence may well have been more harmful still. I would say that on balance Kellam was right in calling Ricky to the stand.

Q: Do you think the defense made *any* errors?

A: Yes, some minor ones during the trial and two major ones before that. I believe that with the kids Kellam should have pursued certain lines of questioning much further than he did, thereby revealing more blatantly some of the flaws in their testimony. By pressing harder at times, he could have made *all* the jury members recognize those inconsistencies and contradictions that, as it was, seemed to have escaped a few of us. Also, in retrospect, the histrionics he employed during the summation, which I personally found so effective at the time, may well have been too florid for some of the jurors. A cooler approach would have suited them better and it would not have bred the suspicion that Kellam was trying to conceal his client's guilt in a cloud of poetry and tears.

More significant, surely, was Kellam's error in allowing Juror 6 to sit on the jury. I was not present when he was interrogated, but Kellam himself has told me that the prejudice and the stubbornness of this man were plainly evident in his answers to the questions posed. Nevertheless, Kellam did not challenge, because he felt confident that he could "get to" Juror 6, whose intelligence he also discerned and respected. A lawyer can only guess at how a potential juror will think and act in the confines of the jury room; in this instance Kellam, his confidence unfounded, guessed disastrously.

But to me the defense's biggest mistake, although it did not affect the jury's verdict, was made long before the trial began. I confess that I feel I am on unfirm ground in venturing the opinion that Singer should not have requested a Wade Hearing. With no legal background of any kind, I hesitate to challenge the judgment of a professional, and the hearing did, after all, provide a pretrial opportunity for the defense to confront Ricky's accusers. But what a price was paid for a procedure that, in terms of what it proposed to accomplish, was, it seems to me, doomed from the start. The inescapable fact was that Jennifer, Clarissa, and Jimmy had identified as the "perpetrator" a boy they knew from the neighborhood, one whom they had seen countless times. There was no way their identification of Ricky could have been influenced, let alone "tainted," by poor or even fraudulent photographs.

Obviously, my view has the marked advantage of hindsight. At the time Singer petitioned for the hearing he knew far less about the state's case than I know now. Nevertheless, even then the Wade Hearing was a gamble whose loss was virtually assured and the stakes amounted to no less than three additional months for Ricky on Rikers Island. Because the district attorney's office could not locate its star witnessess, the hearing stretched from April until June and the trial was correspondingly delayed.

Q: Taking everything into consideration, how would you then rate the performance of the defense?

A: I think that Kellam and Singer did a superb job overall. Their analysis of the police documents, their organization of the questions and the lines of attack, their conduct of the cross-examinations, their opening statement and summation, their decision to put Ricky on the stand, and the way Kellam questioned him—all demonstrated intelligence, perspicacity, control, aggressiveness, and sensitivity. Not every quality in equal measure perhaps, but enough of each, when each was important, for the defense to have won at least half the battle by the time the jury's deliberations began. At that point the attorneys needed a little help, and because they had made mainly wise decisions during the *voir dire,* they got it.

Q: What happened in the jury room was obviously the high point of the trial for you. How do you see those events now?

A: For me now the deliberations seem to have been a three-act play in which I was a main character; in my own view —though perhaps in no one else's—the hero. In any case, I was certainly subordinate to the heroine, Juror 1. But for sheer theatrical power—the richness of the part—we were both overshadowed by the antagonist, Juror 6. Juror 5, another colorful, meaty role, was also a major character, and the rest of the jurors ranged from featured to barely supporting.

The play began slowly, with much exposition as the jurors examined and discussed the documentary evidence and then, rather haltingly, almost reluctantly, expressed their views. A few people were tentative, guarded, quite deliberately vague; clearly they hoped to make a stand with the majority, but they did not yet know where that stand would be. The two jurors who favored a "guilty" verdict spoke up late, but with such vehemence that bitter conflict was immediately assured. So ended Act I.

Act II saw the "undecideds" gradually, but not too slowly, join the "not guilty" faction. With the formation of a strong majority, the conflict heightened and complications of plot developed: Juror 5's misinterpretation of the evidence, the return to the courtroom to hear the Clarissa tape, the dinner outing, the second return to the courtroom. The characters grew edgier, emotions gained in intensity and in blunt expression. Finally, a climax was reached, and Act II ended, when Juror 5 surrendered to the majority.

The third act was the briefest and the most dramatic. Throughout the focus remained piercingly on Juror 6. From all sides the pressure on him mounted at an irregular but inexorable pace. The pressure was compounded of anger, frustration, and, for some, even despair—and it was all exerted on that one obdurate but vulnerable character. Until at last he exploded, submitted, collapsed, and resolution achieved, the play was over.

Q: As a vehicle to achieve justice, rather than theater, what do you think of the jury?

A: We were, above all else, a responsible, almost extravagantly serious group. If I may refer to "the play" just once more, it had hardly any comic relief. Right from the start all of us were united in one belief at least—that we had been chosen to perform a formidable, indeed fearful, task, and to it we had to apply whatever wisdom we possess.

We were to decide not merely where and how a seventeen-year-old boy would spend the next five to ten or twenty years, but also whether or not he was to be marked for life as a murderer. The decision each one of us made was determined by much more than what we heard and observed in the courtroom. The influences on that decision included all the values and experiences and hopes and suspicions and ideas and ideologies that we carried into the jury room as unseen baggage. This is of course how juries are intended to work. What Mendelow cited as our "sophistication" he would have been better advised to call our humanity, and it was not only inevitable, it was *proper* that this humanity, with all its strengths and failings, be brought to bear on the matter at hand.

Strengths and failings our jury had in abundance. We were not a highly educated group; I'm sure that fewer than half of us had attended college. But almost all of us had basically sound judgment—common sense, if you will. A good many of us had compassion and even more had patience. A few of us were articulate, a few analytical and highly logical in our thinking. A very few of us were forceful and commanding, perhaps not ordinarily but when the challenge to exhibit those qualities finally arose.

We also had our share of ignorance, selfishness, and extreme egotism. But there is no question that our major failing was prejudice. It infected us *all* to varying degrees, but where it was strongest it became the flint from which the spark of disagreement flew.

Ironically, I think now that where the jury is most to be commended was in the painfully conscious effort nearly all of us made to look beyond our prejudices. When, early in the deliberations, Juror 6 said that he was sorry there were no blacks on the jury, to lend us some insight into how "they" think, he was giving voice to a factual observation that probably disturbed everyone: we were a lily-white group sitting in judgment on a young black man. Ricky says he never worried about this and the outcome of the trial proves that he was right not to be concerned. But I doubt that he fully appreciates *why* he was "safe" with us. One of the prime reasons was a peculiar type of backlash, which was evident in the general reaction to Juror 6's early statement: the multivoiced protests that it did not matter that there were no blacks among us, that we were all capable of viewing and judging the evidence fairly. In other words, we were out to prove that our prejudices could be overcome. And although at times they leaked or burst from our words, prove it we did.

Q: All of you?

A: Ten of us anyway. Obviously the rigid resistance of the two holdouts was occasioned by deep-seated feelings—fear, perhaps hatred—toward blacks. As they eventually admitted, their certainty of Ricky's guilt rested not on any evidence or testimony as such, but on Ricky himself. They had "gut feelings" and they sensed "bad vibes." Juror 6 propounded the theory that the defendant and his three accusers were all "in it" together—that is, all the blacks involved were guilty. When, time after time, the holdouts' feeble arguments were countered by a rational look at the facts available to us, the two men retreated into the kind of subjectivity—"I just looked at him and could tell he was guilty"—that reason is powerless to attack.

So, no, not all of us rose above our prejudices. Of the two who did not, at least one finally allowed himself to see that blackness was not the only operative factor in the case. The other, Juror 6, remained convinced to the end that Ricky was guilty. Presumably he thinks so even today. When he eventually collapsed, he claimed he was reacting to group pressure, the weight of which he could no longer sustain. It is regrettable, in a way, that we were able to reach our verdict only by resorting to emotional force, regrettable that, apparently, we could not persuade our last holdout to understand the justness of our decision, regrettable that we could not help him recognize the existence of that greater-than-reasonable doubt. But of course, group pressure is also built into the system. And if it must be used, so be it.

Q: You mention the system. On the basis of your service on this jury, what are your thoughts about the jury system in criminal cases?

A: Because in the Mathes trial the state's case was weak and the defense was skillful, it is, I believe, dangerous for me to generalize from this one experience. The challenge we faced was not severe, in spite of our ten hours of deliberation and conflict. If I venture some opinions, it is with a warning that they may not apply to trials in which defense and prosecution are more evenly matched or in which an elusive truth must be found before a verdict can be reached.

Criticism of the jury system usually centers on the folks in the jury box. Said Jerry Paul, attorney for Joan Little, "A jury box is twelve people deciding who has the 'best lawyer.' "

Wrote Morton Hunt in *The Mugging*, "[A jury is] a collection of persons of no special training or knowledge, no notable intellectuality, no particular awareness of the problems at issue, no strong ideology, no previous trial experience, and no clear ideas about the causes or control of crime. The principal qualification of the ideal juror is that he be an ignoramus about all the subjects to be discussed in the case at hand, and thoroughly underqualified to make expert judgments about the evidence he will be hearing."

I daresay those are not inaccurate descriptions of juries. Certainly the twelve of us did not comprise any kind of elite. While a few of us read newspapers or even books at almost every opportunity and one of us was a whiz at needlepoint and someone else was a great opera buff and a third person claimed to be an expert on *everything*, we would be more appropriately characterized as "salt of the earth" types than as eggheads hatched in sociology, law, or political science. And we did have a pronounced tendency to make judgments on and comparisons of the defense and prosecuting attorneys. But in having said all this, we have neglected the salient point: The hallmark of the jury system is the ordinariness of the people in the jury box.

As we were constantly reminded during the *voir dire* and the judge's charge to the jury, it was our function to decide on the *facts* of the case, or, to use a grander term, the truth. (As a practical matter, for us this reduced to judging the credibility of the state's star witnesses; that was essentially all we had to do.) We were not to be concerned with the refinements of the law—for example, whether Darrell Mathes should have been indicted on a charge of first- rather than second-degree murder —or the severity of the sentence the defendant faced if he was found guilty. And if the jury's role is restricted to assessing the evidence that has been presented to it—to determining what parts of that evidence are valid and what parts are suspect— then, usually, the need for expertise vanishes and the common sense that I believe distinguished our jury becomes all that matters.

True, the common sense of a jury is not guaranteed. In selecting jury members, prosecution and/or defense may err. Indeed, it is established practice for either side, intent above all else on winning its case, to seek among potential jurors not necessarily those who seem most intelligent, but those who are most likely to hold advantageous prejudices. The adversary nature of the selection process should serve to lessen the possibility of empaneling a jury that is predisposed toward one side or the other. In any case, another factor is at work here: the unpredictability of the human animal.

Who would have guessed that an unemployed middle-aged blue-collar worker, living in a crime-ridden city and enraged by the smart-ass young punks and welfare chiselers who are invading his neighborhood, would decline an opportunity to put a swaggering, hostile black adolescent behind bars for a few years? A juror of ours who meets that description did—and without a moment of hesitation or reluctance. Who would have suspected that a man who, less than twenty-five years ago, fled to freedom from a Communist-controlled Eastern European country would have fully embraced the bigotry inherent in the equation black equals guilt? That describes one of our worthies too. Who would have imagined that a pleasant, demure, pretty young speech therapist would assume control of a group of eleven people, all older than she—some considerably so—and guide them to her goal with such wit, subtlety, charm, and power that at times she seemed a veritable Joan of Arc? Our forewoman takes those honors.

So jurors may surprise you. Of course, no one, in or out of a jury room, is capable of complete reversal of his or her nature. In the deepest sense, the words and actions of all twelve of us were totally compatible with the ideas and personalities we brought to the trial. But it was not in the deepest sense—on the contrary, it was only in the most superficial sense—that the attorneys could even hope to know us.

Beyond unpredictability is the capacity to rise to a challenge. Serving on the jury was exactly that to each of us; we all recognized that more was being demanded of us—in the way of wisdom, if nothing else—than had often—perhaps ever—been demanded of us before. Some of us were almost embarrassed to be in the position we were. Some of us, when the deliberations grew fierce, were afraid. As we had been warned repeatedly during the *voir dire*, this was not Perry Mason stuff. Anyone who might have waited for the real murderer of Edward Fendt to be suddenly and dramatically exposed would have waited in vain. But we were too serious, too dedicated, even to entertain such thoughts. There was never a time during the deliberations when we lost sight of the reality that confronted us. And for me there was never a time when I doubted that all of us—the holdouts included—were trying to deal with that reality as responsibly as our intelligence and our human understanding allowed.

To paraphrase Bernard Shaw's Eliza Doolittle, the difference between an ordinary man and a juror is not how he behaves, but how he's regarded. This, it seems to me, is the key to the success of the jury system in criminal trials. If a person, whatever his background, knows that much is expected of him —no less than helping to determine the course of someone else's life—in all probability that person will strive with all his capability to be wise and just and compassionate, to stretch himself beyond his foibles and his prejudices. One thing you can be sure of: he will not forget that the stakes are high.

Q: Your jury determined the course of Ricky Mathes's life. You set him free. Looking to the future, what can we expect he will do with his freedom?

A: First of all, except for derelicts in the wintertime, freedom is always to be preferred to imprisonment. Ricky admits that there are boys on Rikers Island who are better housed, clothed, and fed in the ARDC than they would be in their own homes. But not one of them, he claims—and who can doubt him?—would reject an opportunity to walk out of there today. In our society the desire for freedom is ubiquitous and all-powerful, and in granting Ricky his, the jury gave him not only what I think he deserves, but what, long ago, he was promised. But the question is what will he do with his freedom? For that matter, what has he been doing with it? The answer carries us away from lofty concepts such as justice and birthright and leaves us in the streets of a ghetto.

There was jubilation the night he was acquitted. Ricky, his father, assorted brothers, sisters, and other relatives drove from the courtroom to the South Jamaica home of his aunt and uncle. The party began just before midnight and continued for hours. But the next morning Ricky was back on 201st Place in St. Albans and things were no better than they had been in the days following his mother's death a year before. In fact, some of the amenities were gone. The Mathes car sat moldering in the garage, its motor shot. And the telephone had been removed.

Thus, when late in the afternoon Leroy Kellam had an important message for Ricky, he couldn't call but had to drive the few blocks from his office to the Mathes house. Ricky listened with surprise, and perhaps a momentary thrill, as Kellam explained that he had just received a phone call from a juror who was planning to write a book about the trial. He wanted Ricky's cooperation in answering questions about his life both before and after his arrest. It could take many, many hours, stretching over a long period, and Ricky would be paid for his help by sharing in the proceeds from the book. He agreed immediately, without any hesitation, drove with Kellam back to the law office, and soon after was on the phone with the juror, saying yes, he would do it—yes, he would try very hard to remember his childhood—no, he wouldn't mind talking about Rikers Island—yes, he knew which one the eleventh juror was. "I'll never forget any of you," he said.

Within a few days he met the juror and his family, accepted without comment and with only a nod the terms of payment, and arranged for the first interview, which then took place in late October. It was followed by many others, extending through the rest of the fall and into the winter and the spring. In the beginning he and the juror met weekly. He didn't mind talking and trying to dredge up his past. At times he enjoyed some good laughs. But the idea of being the subject of a book never really excited him. It didn't "turn him on" the way it did his family. It was just something to do.

And the fact was there was little else to do. In the first months after his acquittal it was pleasant just to sit around the house after sleeping until noon or later. He knew he would have to return to school sometime, but never again, he vowed, to Andrew Jackson. It was good to be back with his girlfriends, particularly Lala. He spent a lot of time at her house, after she got home from school. He continued with the writing that he had started on Rikers Island. On the first and last Sundays of every month, he attended meetings of the 5 Per Cent Nation, at temples in the Bronx and Brooklyn as well as in Queens. Like the telephone, the basket on the garage in the backyard was missing, so he wasn't playing much basketball. Mainly he was just hanging around.

Winter came. The interviews for the book were much less frequent. He caught a cold and was sick for a week. He developed a rash on his hand. But in February he started school—night school; he was aiming for a high-school-equivalency diploma, but with all those "clowns" in the classroom it was hard to learn. He did go back to Andrew Jackson, a couple of times a week, to play basketball in the community center. He broke up with Lala—she was too possessive—but they made up again a few weeks later.

In the spring his eldest sister, Penny, gave birth to her second child, a girl, and soon she and her kids moved out of the house in St. Albans to her own place in Far Rockaway. Shortly before the end of the term, Ricky dropped out of night school —he wasn't learning anything, he claimed. Lala was sent off to Oklahoma to stay with her grandparents. There was less to do than ever. He and his younger brother, Lewis, put the basket back on the garage. He asked around about a summer job, a permanent job, a part-time job, any kind of job. With no success. And by spring's end the interviews were over.

This is what Ricky has done with his freedom so far. What will he do with it in the future? With help from a friend of Kellam's he hopes to enter an electronics training school in the fall, to learn how to repair TVs and radios and stereos. There could be a problem here in that he may not have passed, or even taken, the necessary high school math courses. He will have to wait and see. Beyond that he has no plans. His dream of attending college and going on to become a pro basketball player has apparently been abandoned. If you were to ask him what happened to the dream, he would shrug his shoulders, perhaps smile, though just as likely not, and answer plaintively, "I dunno."

Q: Why are Ricky's present and future so bleak?

A: Sometime in the past—I'm sure it was long before his arrest—Ricky lost the drive and the animation that almost all youngsters have. I can only speculate as to why: the possible reasons range from his experiences within the family to his perceptions of black and white society. But whatever the reasons, he has been left introverted, passive, indifferent, without motivation or direction or energy. There is crime all around him but, probably because of his mother's influence and that of the 5 Per Cent Nation, he has rejected that path. No other paths are clearly defined or especially inviting. The 5 Per Cent Nation, girls, basketball—they all have their attractions and if he drops one or the other for a time, he will no doubt soon return to it, out of boredom if nothing else. But for him there is no real spark of excitement anywhere.

In his lack of responsibility, Ricky is like a child. In his resignation, he is like an old man. Where is his youth? His manhood? He must be capable of deep feeling, but what can arouse it? Or why does he hide it? The jury returned him to freedom. What will bring him back to life?

Q: Are these the final questions?

A: Yes, and I have no answers.

Epilogue

WHEN, on the evening of the first day of the trial, I started keeping a journal, I had no thought that it would eventually lead to the writing of a book. Similarly, when the idea for the book came to me, I only dimly foresaw the problems I would encounter in researching the background of the trial. Leroy Kellam offered me his enthusiastic cooperation from the start, including full access to the defense files. And of course, his client, Ricky Mathes, seemed at first just as willing to give me all the information I needed from him, at least to the extent his memory allowed. He understood that his role in the project was indispensable: without his full commitment to it, there could be no book.

I hit my first stumbling block when I wrote to Assistant District Attorney Bernard Mendelow requesting an interview. I asked for as little as an hour of his time, just long enough for me to pose a few key questions, the answers to which, I explained, I considered essential to the balance, accuracy, completeness, and objectivity of the book. Mendelow called me within a day after he received my letter. He was gracious in his refusal: while he would like very much to help me, he said, his superiors had "instructed" him not to speak to me. I persisted. Might I perhaps submit questions to him in writing, which he could then answer at his convenience and discretion? He agreed to go back to his superiors and sound them out once more. A few days later, Mendelow telephoned me again. Our conversation this time was shorter and more abrupt. He was sorry, but under no circumstances could I interview him. Period (as Ricky would say).

His rebuff proved to be but the first disappointment handed down to me by the Queens district attorney's office. I could manage without Mendelow, I decided, hoping that in the mass of material his office had turned over to the defense months before I could uncover some further justification for the prosecution's case and some insights into their strategy. The material was, for the most part, filed away in Stephen Singer's office. Singer, who was easily as cooperative as Kellam, let me have everything, including an index he had prepared that summarized all the police documents and indicated their comparative value for defense purposes. The index was invaluable to me, as were many of the documents. But the defense files held nothing to reinforce or even to illuminate the state's case against Ricky.

Nor did the defense file contain any of the pictures that Kellam had submitted to the jury—the photographs of the crime scene and the line-up, the snapshots of Ricky taken at the funeral parlor, the police sketch shown on CBS News. Although these were all defense exhibits, and stamped as such by the clerk of the court at the time they were entered into the trial as evidence, they had not been returned to Kellam or Singer after the trial was over. The defense attorneys surmised that they had been given to the D.A.'s office. This was an ominous note, but in spite of it I was determined to see the pictures again.

Thus there ensued a month-long campaign to gain access to the district attorney's file on Darrell Mathes. Because, by that time, the trial had been over for more than three months, because legally the state was prevented from either appealing the verdict or retrying Ricky for the same crime, because I was seeking *defense* exhibits, and because New York State has a Freedom of Information Act that the lawyers believed applied here, I did not expect to face stiff resistance in my second appeal to the prosecution. How wrong I was. In person and by telephone, and with vigorous help from both defense attorneys, I tried repeatedly and fruitlessly to get permission to view the file.

Eventually I discovered the reason for my failure: The D.A.'s office knew that I was writing a book (thanks, no doubt, to my letter to Mendelow) and suspected that it would put them in an "unfavorable light." This Singer learned from an assistant district attorney and the view was later confirmed and elaborated upon by a high-level member of the D.A.'s staff in a conversation with Kellam: not only would the book be damaging, but the author was guilty of fraud. It seems the D.A.'s office had decided I had lied during the *voir dire* when, in answer to that question of Mendelow's, I had said I was not a writer. I *was* a writer, it was charged. Moreover, from the outset it was my intention to get on the jury in order to write a book about the trial. Implicit in this accusation was another innuendo: that as a juror I began with a prejudice in favor of the defendant.

Had anyone ever sued the district attorney's office for slander? Successfully? I was irate but I did not lose my head. After all, the charges were made during a telephone conversation, unbugged and untaped, between Kellam and the D.A.'s aide. The latter, if and when the time came, would surely deny the whole thing. I had no case.

But I still had the challenge. At the suggestion of the defense attorneys, I wrote another letter, this time going directly to the top, the Honorable Nicholas Ferraro himself, District Attorney of Queens County. Making no reference to the accusations that had been leveled against me, I asked, first, that he countermand the instructions preventing me from interviewing Mendelow. I knew I didn't stand a chance on that one—but there was no harm in trying. Moreover, by making two requests, I thought I was more likely to gain agreement to the second: an opportunity to examine the state's file on the case.

Like my letter to Mendelow, my letter to Ferraro was never answered in writing. After a week of silence, word reached me through Kellam that the district attorney had approved my request to see the file. (My request for an interview with Mendelow was simply ignored.) I was to call one of his aides to set up an appointment.

Four or five phone calls and more than three weeks later, I finally entered the office of a chief assistant to the district attorney. His secretary, who was suffering from a terrible cold, greeted me pleasantly and proceeded to advise me of her instructions and mine: I could not remove the file from her desk; I could not look through the file; I could not take notes; I could not extract any item from the file; I could not make photocopies of any documents. I could merely ask the secretary for specific items and she would sift through the file material and try to find them for me. If she succeeded she would hand them to me, permit me to scrutinize them for a while, and then take them back and return them to where they belonged.

This farcical *modus operandi* broke down almost as soon as it was attempted. Perhaps if she had not been plagued by that cold, the secretary would have tried harder to adhere to the established rules. As it was, I had somewhat freer access to the file than was officially decreed. In any event, it was all for almost naught. As I have previously noted, I found in the file nothing new to implicate Ricky in the Edward Fendt murder. And aside from a few photographs of the slain victim and of the bullet-ridden potato chip truck, I did not find the evidential pictures either. I returned all five pounds of the file to the secretary, thanked her and wished her a speedy recovery, and left, to continue my search elsewhere.

The pictures were finally located at central Police Headquarters in Manhattan. The other material never did turn up because, I am sure, it does not exist. The state disclosed to the jury all the evidence it had. The resistance I encountered in trying to research this book served only to confirm my view that the state's case was shamefully feeble. If Mendelow had won the verdict, wouldn't his door have been open to me? If Ricky had had a long arrest record not revealed in court, wouldn't the file have been more readily available? And I wonder sometimes: if the three kids had identified a white boy in the same way they identified Ricky, wouldn't there have been no trial at all?

I found scarcely anything of value in the D.A.'s file on the case, but a few months later I did come across a pertinent statement by an assistant attorney general of the United States, the head of the Justice Department's Criminal Division. Speaking to a group of criminal lawyers, he said:

> As prosecutors, we can never hesitate to follow the evidence wherever it leads—regardless of to whom it may point. . . . But at the same time, we must never seek to carry investigations and prosecutions beyond where the evidence may lead, for personal reasons or for prospects of political, economic or other advancement. *The courage to prosecute when the evidence is there must always be matched by a recognition of the responsibility not to prosecute when the evidence is lacking.*

The italics are mine.

If the district attorney's office offered me almost no cooperation, there were other employees of the Queens County Criminal Court who were more than eager to be of assistance. In their own small ways they were as helpful as Leroy Kellam and Steve Singer were in large and crucial ones. I had help, too, from people at WCBS-TV News and at New York City's Department of Correction. It was through the latter office that I got authorization to visit the Adolescent Reception Detention Center on Rikers Island.

Whatever favorable impressions I carried away from the institution probably derived from the warmth and the decency of the man who was my guide there. It is a comfortless, embattled place (where four outbreaks of violence have occurred in the three months since my visit, two pitting black against Puerto Rican inmates, the other two, inmates against CO's), and a good many of the staff members seem to view visitors with the same suspicion that the inmates exhibit toward everyone except their "brothers." But my guide was different. He exchanged friendly greetings with several of the inmates we passed in the corridors and he spoke of the young men with understanding, even with hope, and without fear, hostility, or contempt. True, he does not gaze upon them for hours from a glass-enclosed observation booth at the end of a quad; nor does he attempt to maintain order and develop reading skills in a classroom. If he did, perhaps he would become as tough and embittered and rigidly bureaucratic as those who do. But I was glad to have found him there nevertheless. Gentle and compassionate, he would appear an uncommon man anywhere. On Rikers Island, perpetually on the verge of siege, he moved as a man of peace among armies preparing for war.

When an amateur writes a book, you can be sure he will be barraged with advice and comment from relatives, friends, and, to use Ricky's phrase, "good acquaintances." Their suggestions may be practical in nature but contradictory ("Get yourself a little office somewhere" versus "You can work at home and save all that traveling time." "Take six months off from work and do it right" versus "Evenings and weekends for a year should be enough. After all, there's no need to rush to finish it—it isn't going to be *timely*"); or they may be dangerous ("You should try to interview the kids"); or they may be *intentionally* funny ("Maybe Wise will chip in and help promote the book").

The words will differ, of course, but remarks of this nature are sure to greet the first-time author whatever his or her subject may be. But embark upon a book about crime in New York, about a murder committed in the course of an armed robbery, about a seventeen-year-old black defendant who could be "put away" for twenty-five years, and you are apt to hear words that sound a darker and more disturbing note. Earlier I mentioned that the question I am most frequently asked when people learn the outcome of the trial is some variation of "Was the kid really innocent?" What has shocked me most, however, is the number of people who, whether they ask the question or not, are positive of the answer.

They may know nothing else about the case, but once they know the color of the defendant, they are convinced he is guilty. There is not a George Wallace supporter among them and all of them would deny, with varying degrees of vehemence, that they are infected with bigotry. They would use words like "rational," "thoughtful," "informed," and "sophisticated" to describe themselves. A few might even try on "liberal" for size. But in the time and place and climate of opinion in which they—and I—live, a suspicion of guilt directed at a black becomes for them a fact of guilt, and any opportunity to pull a potential mugger off the streets is too urgent to be denied.

These people who tell me, smilingly or not, that I and the others on the jury made a serious mistake—all of them share a belief that only one of them actually voiced: when blacks are involved, where there is smoke there has to be fire. Just as I can never hope to convince them that Ricky was innocent, I am powerless to make them realize that their belief, and the intensity with which they hold it, are part of the problem. They are contributing, in their own insidious fashion, to the endless cycle of fear and discrimination and violence. They help to ensure that the smoke continues to rise and the fires continue to burn.

But the great majority of the people I know are not racists, and allowing for a touch of skepticism here and there, after listening to the details of the trial they accept the jury's verdict as just. A good many deplore the fact that Ricky spent eleven months on Rikers Island and some show genuine concern as to what he has been doing since his acquittal. Nevertheless, the experience of writing this book has demonstrated to me how steeped even the best of us whites are in the stereotypes that doom racial understanding.

I recall remarks made by two people whose commitment to the cause of civil rights is unquestioned and whose very jobs, either directly or indirectly, are benefiting blacks. When I told one of them that I had given Ricky a portion of the manuscript of this book to read, she asked, neither in jest nor in conscious derogation, "You mean he can read?" Said another friend, upon hearing that Ricky's sister was pregnant, "Maybe he's the father."

Since I have come to know the Matheses, I have emphasized to everyone who expresses interest that here is a family, whatever its problems, that resists stereotypes: they are not on welfare, they own their own home, the father has held the same good job for almost twenty years, the family remained together until very recently, Ricky was not a gang member and he did not have any sort of police record—until he was arrested a month after his sixteenth birthday. But those last nine words condemn him. They act as a trigger to set off all the "certainties" that define lower-class blacks for us. And Ricky immediately becomes one of "them."

"Them" and "they." Pronouns without antecedents, thus automatically referring to blacks, they have pelted me from all sides ever since I took my seat in the jury box. Starting with a few of my fellow jurors—most notably Juror 6—I have encountered a veritable brain trust of authorities, white to a man, on the behavior of black people. The generalizations I have heard on how "they" think and act and believe are wide-ranging, precise, and comprehensive, and they are delivered with supreme assurance. The self-proclaimed experts are always as confident as they are well-meaning; their knowledge derives from various sources, especially of course from their own experience; and their pronouncements cannot be casually dismissed —somewhere, I think, they must contain truth.

And so I listen carefully, appreciatively, to my expert friends, aware that it is their aim—and how earnestly they hold it—to illuminate Ricky for me. And I find that as I listen he grows increasingly obscure, fading into a high school class of "underachievers," or into a group of tenement-dwellers in the East Bronx. For the history teacher does not know Ricky and neither does the realty agent. And therefore, ultimately, their generalizations prove to be a barrier, a barrier to the understanding of any one person, a barrier to my understanding of the defendant.

The defendant, my "coauthor." No problem I faced in researching this book was as frustrating as dealing with Ricky Mathes. From the moment of our first meeting, I strove to build the mutual trust without which our relationship was sure to be barren. In the beginning it seemed to me that my efforts were succeeding, at least to a limited degree. During our early inter-

views, as guarded and taciturn as Ricky was, he conveyed the
impression that he was genuinely trying to remember and to
communicate. He even claimed to be enjoying these sessions,
although I knew they were difficult for him. Indeed, they would
be difficult for any seventeen-year-old boy who was asked to
mine from his past the events that had shaped him and to tell
them to a comparative stranger. And to Ricky, I thought, I must
appear as not only a stranger, but a stranger from another
world. By all surface factors, this gulf between us was too enormous to contemplate, but it was just a matter of time, I judged,
before it would be bridged.

Time passed—and the gulf seemed to remain as it was. In
the third and fourth interviews Ricky was no more self-reveal-
ing than he had been in the first and second. The brief, mumbled answers that I had accepted then were less tolerable now.
How many times would I have to hear "I dunno," "I can't
remember," "It was awright," "That's how I am"? Where was
the spark of interest, the burst of enthusiasm that would shed
some light or, if only momentarily, penetrate that fog of passivity? Was there no way I could move him or touch him?

After six "working" meetings, spanning nearly two months,
and about ten hours of taped interviews (much of our conversation went deliberately unrecorded), I concluded, resignedly,
that I had learned as much about Ricky as I ever could. If he
remained an enigma to me in many ways, I was prepared to
accept that, consoling myself with the thought that no one ever
truly "knows" anyone else. If I had failed to pierce his defenses
and thereby reach the real Ricky, I was prepared to accept that
disappointment too. After all, I brought to this challenge neither the background of a reporter nor the training of a psy-
chologist, and for my efforts I had in fact gathered a substantial
amount of material for the book.

So I began writing and Ricky and I saw much less of each
other. Then, gradually and to my increasing surprise, I found
myself knowing him better. As I listened to the tapes, I realized
just how much he *had* told me. I could perceive the influences
on his life and could trace them to the young man he had

become. I could appreciate the pattern and the texture of the stories he had told. And while Ricky took on shape and dimension and clarity, I recognized the source of my earlier frustration: chained to the values and the experiences of my own past, I had sought in Ricky what I could expect to find in a white, middle-class adolescent. I could probably find the qualities in many blacks of Ricky's age too. But the drive, the urge to experience, the will to accomplish, the capacity for excitement—these I could not find in Ricky because either they were not there or they were buried so deep that, for now at least, they were beyond detection.

As I was reaching this understanding, however, another source of frustration emerged and this has haunted my relationship with Ricky ever since. Because he does not have a telephone, I can communicate with him in a limited number of ways, all equally unsatisfactory: I can try to reach him through Leroy Kellam, whose office is just blocks away from the Mathes house; but this is an imposition I must reserve for emergencies. I can drive over to his house, but then I face the possibility of not finding him at home or of intruding on his family's privacy. I can write him a letter, but then I have no guarantee that he will answer.

At one time or another I have reached Ricky by each of these methods, but the fact remains that since we abandoned our regularly scheduled meetings, communication with him has been chancy and sporadic at best. Repeatedly he agrees to meet me at a specified time and place and fails to show up. Repeatedly he promises to call me and the phone doesn't ring. And then, unexpectedly—because I have learned to *expect* nothing from him—he will appear, and always with an explanation for the broken engagements and the unplaced telephone calls.

Many times while I was writing Ricky's story, I had a need to ask him a few more key questions—to clarify an incident, to fill in a blank, to elaborate on a point. Eventually I got all the answers he could supply, but accomplishing that proved far more difficult in the last months than I would have predicted in the early days of our relationship.

Today, as far as the book is concerned, there is no necessity for Ricky and me to meet ever again. It is too late for him to add anything and it is highly unlikely that he has anything to add. The questions that remain in my mind he cannot answer. The business matters in which we are involved can be handled by mail. Nevertheless, I am almost certain that I will continue to see Ricky, however irregularly and unpredictably. For one thing, I want to; if to me his future is a dismal blur, I am all the more anxious to know what he will be doing next month or next year or a decade from now. Furthermore, I suspect that he will want to see me. Although I cannot believe, as much as I would like to, that I ever succeeded in creating that relationship of deep mutual trust, I do believe that we have shared so much— he has told me so much—that there exists between us now a bond not easily broken. Besides, we had a *few* enjoyable times together.

It is fitting, I think, that I should end with some of these times. In a personal reminiscence that dwells on difficulties, obstacles, disappointments, and frustrations, some attention to pleasant memories is surely in order.

There was the moment Ricky walked into my office after I had not seen him in almost two months and had just about given up on him. He doesn't often smile, but his grin that morning reached from ear to ear. He was so obviously tickled to have surprised me that I could only sit back and laugh.

There was the "extra" work that Ricky did for me on the book—taking trips to the library to locate and photocopy newspaper articles, making Xerox copies of the pages of this manuscript and collating them—all done willingly, indeed eagerly, and without error.

There were the lunches we had together, when Ricky would relax and just talk, not for the book and certainly not of himself, but about the "doings" of his friends.

There were the times Ricky played host to me and members of my family; whenever we visited him, whether the purpose was "business" or social, he served us graciously, generously—above all, proudly.

And there was, finally, that one special visit and the best memory of all—Christmas Eve, when my wife, my daughter, and I called at the Mathes house to deliver some presents. There were a couple for Ricky himself, one of which we had talked about and he expected, and a little surprise for the family. Robert Mathes was there, as were Ricky's younger brother, Lewis, and his sisters Penny and Sheila, who were decorating the Christmas tree. We all sat around chatting for a while and then, suddenly, Ricky reached under the tree and brought forth a gold-and-white-striped box. Almost awkwardly he thrust it at me. "This is for you," he said, and he started to smile. Unlike the Mathes family, I could not wait for Christmas morning. I had to open the box immediately, with Ricky standing over me, watching and beaming.

His gift to me was a brocade necktie. It was solid black.

New York City
August, 1976

Aftermath

ON JANUARY 25, 1977, more than five months after I had finished the Epilogue and about two months after this book had first gone to press, Darrell Mathes was arrested for attempted murder.

It was, like my first day in court, a Tuesday. At about 6 P.M., Ricky called me at the office (he knows I work late). When I asked how he was, he answered, "Terrible." I felt a tremor of fear, knowing immediately that he was in serious trouble. In the past, no matter how discouraged he might have been at any particular time, Ricky had always assured me he was "awright."

"What's wrong?" I asked.

"I was arrested."

The tremor became a chill.

"For what?"

His reply was like an electric shock: "Attempted murder."

For a moment I couldn't speak; then I asked, "Did you do it?"

He answered my question with one of his own: "Do I look like it?" There was a note of impatience in his voice.

"I have to ask that question," I said.

"I know, I know," he replied. The impatience was gone.

When I asked him exactly what had happened, he explained that over the weekend a man of about twenty-six who lives diagonally across the street from the Mathes house had been shot. Ricky had heard about it and had noticed the cops around the crime scene, but that was all he had known until his arrest that morning. He was calling me from Queens Central Booking, at the same 112th Precinct in Forest Hills where he had spent that Sunday evening twenty-six months before.

I asked if he had called Mr. Kellam. No, this call to me was the first he had been allowed to make. "O.K.," I said, "I'll phone him right away." It flashed through my mind then that I should end our conversation with the useless advice that seems most appropriate for such occasions—"Stay cool" or "Just relax" or "Try not to worry because everything's going to be all right"— but in my agitated state such words refused to come. I could say only an abrupt goodbye and hang up.

I called Kellam at home and told him what I had just learned; at once I experienced a rush of relief as I transferred at least part of the burden from my shoulders to his. He accepted it without pause or question, saying he would phone Central Booking to find out whatever he could and would call me back. I put down the phone and for several minutes I stared into space. I thought about this book and the ramifications of the new arrest. I was suddenly conscious of my presumption in asking Kellam to defend Ricky again—I was not the "court" and had no authority to name an attorney—but then I quickly realized that I had not *asked* him to do anything: I had merely assumed he would take the case, and my assumption had proved justified. Mainly, as I waited for Kellam's call, I thought of Ricky—and once more wanted desperately to be able to penetrate his mind.

Kellam phoned me within ten minutes. He added one highly significant fact to what Ricky had told me: Joseph Mathes had been arrested for attempted murder along with his brother. Kellam said they were expected to be in night court by 9 P.M. I arranged to meet him there.

The courtroom, in the same Queens County Criminal Court Building, was much smaller than the one I had come to know so well. This chamber was narrow and it had no jury box. All decisions were made by the judge alone, and he made them in what seemed to me the most routine, perfunctory fashion. The defendants who stood before him in turn—every one of them a teen-age male—were either remanded to Rikers Island or conditionally released in the custody of their parents; most of the hearings were concluded within two or three minutes. That is, until the clerk of the court summoned Darrell and Joseph Mathes.

Before they were brought in, Kellam, who was defending Ricky only (Joe was represented by a Legal Aid attorney), had shown me a copy of the felony complaint. On the basis of testimony given to a detective by the victim while in the hospital, the defendants were charged with attempted murder in the second degree and illegal possession of a weapon. The warrant supplied only the sparsest details of the incident: The victim stated that at his home on Saturday evening, January 22, at about eight twenty-five, he was shot in the side by a bullet from a .32-caliber pistol, and he identified his assailants as Darrell and Joseph Mathes.

They were led into the courtroom and stood at the bar. The clerk read the charge. Kellam and the Legal Aid attorney argued that it was physically impossible for *both* the defendants to have shot the victim. Kellam remarked that this was one of the strangest charges he had ever seen—usually, in such cases, one defendant was said to have acted in concert with or as an accomplice to the other. The assistant district attorney countered that the charge was sufficient for this hearing and he emphasized that the victim was still in the hospital suffering from a collapsed lung. "We have a near homicide here, Your Honor," he concluded. The judge nodded, imposed bail at ten thousand dollars for each, set January 28 as the date for the hearing, and remanded the brothers to Rikers Island. The arraignment and bail setting took less than ten minutes. Then, as Robert Mathes had, 26 months earlier, I watched the court officers lead Ricky away.

At some point in the middle of the arraignment, while Joe's lawyer was speaking, Ricky had turned slowly around until he had spotted me in the spectator section. He had given me just the barest hint of a smile and then had shrugged his shoulders in a gesture that was sadly familiar to me. In the past, this gesture had said, or had been followed by, "I dunno." Now it carried an added implication: I don't know what they're doing to me.

And so Ricky maintained when he phoned me from court a few minutes after I returned home. While waiting for the police van to take him to the ARDC, he had received permission to make a call. He again claimed to have no knowledge of the shooting. Indeed, he barely knew—had never even spoken to—the victim. Why, then, would this man falsely identify him? Ricky had no idea. Stupidly I reminded him that he had once vowed to me that he would never return to Rikers Island. "Do you think I *want* to go there?" he asked. Anyway, he needed money. He asked me to withdraw some from his bank account —jointly established in his name and mine with his share of the advance on this book—and get it to him through Mr. Kellam. He had to buy cigarettes and other supplies at the ARDC "commissary." He ended the conversation quite suddenly—actually, in midsentence. "I have to go now." Presumably the police van had arrived.

I didn't see Ricky again for a week. On January 28, the victim of the shooting was still confined to the hospital and the district attorney's office asked that the hearing be adjourned until the following Tuesday, when it was expected he would be sufficiently recovered from his injury to testify in court. Ricky was brought to the courthouse on the twenty-eighth but he never left the "pen." Through an associate of Kellam's I managed to pass along to him the money he had requested.

The hearing was held on February 1. The victim—tall and robust but, judging from the way he held his right arm to his chest, still suffering some discomfort—was the sole witness. His testimony raised as many questions in my mind as it answered, but there was no denying that it answered the most important question of all: Who had shot him?

He spoke slowly, cautiously, but fluently, and referred to Defendant Subject 1 (Ricky) and Defendant Subject 2 (Joe). His story, as elicited in turn by an assistant district attorney, Kellam, and Joe's Legal Aid lawyer, was brief and uncomplicated:

Between eight-fifteen and eight-thirty on the evening of January 22, there had been a knock on the front door of his house. He went to the door, opened it, and saw three people outside. One, at the bottom of the steps and perhaps even on the sidewalk, he could not see clearly enough ever to identify. The other two were at the top of the steps. The one closest to the door was Joe Mathes, who, the victim rather grudgingly admitted, was an acquaintance. The second, standing to Joe's right and a little farther from the door, he identified as Defendant Subject 1. He knew him by sight, having seen him in the street on several occasions, but not, at that time, by name. The victim asked what the young men wanted. They did not respond. Then he saw in Ricky's hand an object that he thought was a knife. He grabbed for Ricky's arm, whereupon Joe said, "Pop him. Pop him." Ricky fired a gun. The victim felt a stinging pain in his chest. The three men fled. The police were called. End of story.

Attempts by Kellam and the Legal Aid lawyer to elicit additional information were thwarted by the assistant D.A.'s constant objections, sustained by the bench: the questions were not relevant or appropriate to this forum. Just about the only other important facts Kellam was able to educe were that the victim was at no time unconscious and that he had been to Joe's house two or three times over the past year.

With the conclusion of the victim's testimony, the two defense attorneys moved that the charges against their respective clients be dismissed. The judge denied their motions just as routinely as the lawyers had made them. He then ruled that the case be referred to the grand jury and the defendants remanded to custody. The hearing was over.

And the questions remain. As we await the next development—no doubt the grand jury will hand up an indictment—the crime seems to me so strange that it borders on the bizarre and senseless. Sift through the victim's testimony and you find not a single statement that even remotely suggests a motive for the shooting. Aside from asking what they wanted, he claims he had absolutely no conversation with his assailants. Clearly, then, they had not demanded anything of him or tried to enter his house. By quite deliberately minimizing the nature of his relationship with Joe and by affirming that he did not know Ricky, he negates the obvious possibility that "bad blood" or revenge prompted the crime. One must conclude that there was no reason for the shooting—or that the victim's testimony was far from the whole truth.

It is the latter conclusion that is supported by some other curious observations. If the victim had, as he said, recognized Joe immediately and had never lost consciousness, he could have given the police the identity of at least one of his assailants, and could have described the other, on the night of the shooting, before or after he was taken to the hospital. Yet the arrest warrant was not signed until Tuesday, more than two days later. Furthermore, the warrant states that the victim identified Darrell Mathes by name as one of the attempted killers, but at the hearing this man testified that on Saturday night he did not know Darrell's name. Lying in the hospital with his collapsed lung, how had he found it out?

Ricky's alibi once again involves his friends. He says that at about eight-thirty that Saturday night he and a friend were just leaving the apartment of his brother Dwayne's girlfriend. This young woman, whom I have spoken to, confirms the time of Ricky's departure and adds that he and his friend were at her apartment for at least an hour. Ricky goes on to say that as he was walking home (Dwayne's girlfriend lives about two and a half blocks away), he saw cops and a police car in front of the victim's house. After arriving home, he changed his clothes and, with his younger sister Sheila, went off to a neighborhood party, where he stayed until the early hours of Sunday morning. One fact is indisputable: Ricky and Joe remained at home or in the neighborhood from the time of the shooting until the morning of their arrest. There they were, in effect, just waiting for the police to pick them up. Would they have been such sitting ducks had they just shot a man who, they were well aware, could identify one of them by name and the other by sight?

Nevertheless, balancing all the questions that cast doubt on the Mathes brothers' guilt, and looming larger than any of them —perhaps larger than all of them put together—is another question, grim and inescapable: Why would the victim want to frame these young men he barely knows?

It is certainly to be hoped that most, if not all, the questions I raise will someday, somehow, be answered. If not before, then at a trial—to enlighten a jury. Should the case proceed to that point, I have faith that the jury will hear the evidence attentively, will weigh it sensibly, and will arrive at its verdict justly. What I have felt about the jury system stands and it will continue to stand regardless of the outcome of Ricky's second trial.

But meanwhile, I cannot prevent myself from coming to an interim verdict of my own. Admittedly, I can no longer be considered an objective observer. No court in the land would allow me to come within hailing distance of a second Darrell Mathes jury. Another Christmas gift has been added to the black necktie, and many more hours to the time Ricky and I have spent together. He has read, and generally approved, the original manuscript of this book (that is, through the Epilogue). I was at the Mathes house, to give Ricky a copy of the bound galleys, three hours before the shooting occurred. I was the first, the only, person Ricky called from Central Booking.

Recognizing, then, my naked vulnerability, knowing that I am open to charges ranging from blind and baseless and misplaced trust to pathetic naïveté to—vilest of all—bleeding-heart liberalism, I will nonetheless exercise my right to an opinion: I am inclined once again to believe that Ricky is innocent.

My judgment is supported, however insecurely, by the questions and observations that I offered above and by the view of Ricky that I expressed throughout the latter part of this book. To those who argue that, aside from the victim's identification of Ricky, it is highly unlikely that this young man would be unjustly accused of a major felony twice in a period of twenty-six months, I repeat two comments of Kellam's that seem to me singularly pertinent: His logic tells him that if the police can be wrong once, they can just as easily be wrong twice. And recalling with some eloquence the Willard Motley novel and the Humphrey Bogart movie, he contends that he can walk me down streets where you can "knock on any door" and find adolescent boys who, before they are twenty, will be arrested and rearrested and arrested once again, justly and unjustly. They were born to be arrested.

It is this truth that has gripped me most strongly in the days since Ricky's return to Rikers Island. At first his arrest was like a punch that staggered me. I reached out in all directions for supports to steady myself. On the one hand, I felt compelled to do things for him: call Kellam, go to court, speak to the family, get him money. On the other hand, "in the light of the latest developments," I had to review the past, rethink all that I had written, and reconsider all that I had concluded. For reality was suddenly, starkly different.

But was it? What had changed, really? My appraisals of the principals involved in the Potato Chip Murder Trial—of the judge, the attorneys, the jury? No, not one. My impressions of Ricky—most significantly, of his innocence of the first crime? No; I was as deeply convinced of that as ever. Of his future? I had written that it was bleak and dismal—time had merely, if cruelly, proved me right. So except that it now was advisable to change the names of Ricky and his family, not a single sentence of this book has been revised and not a word altered.

I felt, however, that I had an ethical obligation to inform the reader of Ricky's second arrest. As long as the book was not yet published, it seemed fraudulent not to acknowledge it. But a higher morality demanded that the sensational new facts be presented in a way that shifted interest from the obvious, immediate, almost automatic question of "Did he do it?" to the timeless question of "What does it all mean?"

For me Kellam's "knock on any door" remark threw Rickey's arrest into a new perspective. It was, I was now forced to admit, just about inevitable. I had shied away from admitting this to myself before. But given the monotony of his days, the lack of accomplishment, the absence of will, the failure of those around him (including me) to inspire him or lead him, his latest encounter with the law was preordained. That Saturday he had said to me, "I need a job, a job, a job." But I had had no job for him and I knew that, aside from making these periodic pleas to me, he was doing little to find one on his own. He was in fact doing nothing except hanging out on the street—and thereby waiting for the street to claim him as its victim once again.

Kellam cued me into understanding this intellectually. Seeing Ricky at the hearing made me feel it viscerally. He and Joe were led into the courtroom by two uniformed guards and directed to seats in the spectator section across the aisle from me. When one of the guards put his hand on Ricky's arm, Ricky twisted away violently, as if to say, "Get your goddamn hands off me!" Seven nights on Rikers Island had taken their toll. There was nothing like the faint smile and the shrug of the shoulders that had greeted me in night court less than a week earlier. He gave me no more than a quick, blank stare as he took his seat at the far end of the bench next to the wall.

I gazed at him continually during the hearing and gradually I recognized that one aspect of the reality of this book had changed: Ricky was no longer a boy. In the fifteen months since I had first seen him, the tall, skinny seventeen-year-old kid had physically matured into a young man. And the defendant in the murder trial who had looked at his three young accusers—when he had looked at them at all—without apparent emotion or thought, now would not take his eyes off the face of his lone accuser, and his eyes blazed with a hatred I had never seen there before.

Clearly, however, Ricky had hoped—perhaps, naïvely, had even expected—that the judge would approve Kellam's motion to dismiss the charges. When the ruling was otherwise, Ricky grimaced in crushing disappointment and his body sagged. As he was led from the courtroom he did not even glance at me. It was Joe who turned, smiled, and held up two crossed fingers, just before he passed through the doorway of the courtroom and they both disappeared into the "pen."

The next day my education continued. I received a phone call from a social worker at the ARDC. He had a letter from Darrell Mathes to read to me, he said, adding in a slightly puzzled tone, "but it's signed 'Ricky.' " "Yes, that's O.K.," I said. "Go ahead." But in all truth, my first reaction was to wish he hadn't called, to wish there were no letter.

It was, quite simply, a piercing call for help. The repressed anger that I had sensed in Ricky in the courtroom exploded now in a desperate, urgent cry. He was sounding an alarm, for my ears only: "Dear Mel. I can't stand it here this time. I can't tell you how bad it is. I know I was here before but it's much worse now." He went on to say that the police were framing him again and he had to "get back on the street" to fight his case. He had to get out, he repeated—and I had to help him. In closing, he said, "Mel, you know me. You know I won't jump bail. Please help me get out. Love, Ricky."

The letter was short and the Rikers Island social worker read it virtually without pause. I thanked him and asked him to tell Ricky that I would discuss the letter with Mr. Kellam; there was nothing else I could do at this time. Before he hung up, the social worker asked if I was Darrell's lawyer. I answered, "No, just a friend."

So an unfinished story has been brought up to date. Looking to the future, I expect that Ricky will probably be indicted by the grand jury very soon. I am going out to Rikers Island to ask him to meet certain conditions before I will try to do something about raising bail. If he is going to be back on the street, I want to comfort myself with knowing that I've made some effort to keep him out of trouble and, since hope survives, to persuade him to spend his time constructively. I have little reason to feel encouraged, but the fact is that months ago I longed to find a spark of life in Ricky and now I've found rage. Perhaps that is better than nothing.

Someday, of course, he will be back on the street, no matter what. If he meets my conditions, he may be out on bail soon.

Even if he remains on Rikers Island, he will eventually be brought to trial, and whether he is found guilty or innocent, sometime after that he will be free again. There is no denying him his freedom forever, only intermittently. That is why the question of his guilt or innocence fades into an infinitely more commanding issue: There must be a way to reach this young man; there must be an agency or a school or maybe just a person who can reclaim him; there must be a means of seeing that his freedom does not again become an unfolding of emptiness, a succession of days and nights on the street that ultimately ends with a phone call: "I was arrested."

New York City
February 7, 1977

Sha-liek Allah

"Misty Blue"

Rose's are red & violets are blue.
Hate exists in jail & I do too.
But in all reality this can't be true, just.
Misty Blue.
Envy, jealousy & lunacy is here too.
All in the same jail.
What the fuck.
Misty Blue.
If I were a king that sat on a throne.
& had this jail to be my own.
Why! this is what I would do.
Paint it.
Red, Yellow & Orange too.
then give it a sweet name like
Misty Blue.

Peace & Everlasting light
Ricky as Sha-liek
Allah

Rikers Island
February, 1977